# GROWING PAINS

THE HISTORICAL SERIES OF THE REFORMED CHURCH IN AMERICA
IN COOPERATION WITH ORIGINS STUDIES IN
DUTCH AMERICAN HISTORY
NO. 89

# GROWING PAINS
How Racial Struggles Changed
a Church and a School

**Christopher H. Meehan**

WILLIAM B. EERDMANS PUBLISHING COMPANY
Grand Rapids, Michigan / Cambridge, UK

Wm. B. Eerdmans Publishing Co.
2140 Oak Industrial Drive SE, Grand Rapids, Michigan 49505

Cambridge CB3 9PU UK
www.eerdmans.com


Printed in the United States of America

**Library of Congress Cataloging-in-Publication Data**

Cataloging information applied for and in process.

*To my wife, Mary,*
*whose support and love*
*have been bountiful*

## The Historical Series of the Reformed Church in America

The series was inaugurated in 1968 by the General Synod of the Reformed Church in America acting through the Commission on History to communicate the church's heritage and collective memory and to reflect on our identity and mission, encouraging historical scholarship which informs both church and academy.

www.rca.org/series

General Editor
  Rev. Donald J. Bruggink, PhD, DD
  Western Theological Seminary
  Van Raalte Institute, Hope College

Associate Editor
  James Hart Brumm, MDiv
  Blooming Grove, New York
  New Brunswick Theological Seminary

Copy Editor
  JoHannah Smith
  Holland, Michigan

Production Editor
  Russell L. Gasero
  Archives, Reformed Church in America

Commission on History
  James Hart Brumm, MDiv, Blooming Grove, New York
  Lynn Japinga, PhD, Hope College
  David M. Tripold, PhD, Monmouth University
  Douglas Van Aartsen, MDiv, Ireton, IA
  Matthew Van Maastricht, MDiv, Milwaukee, Wisconsin
  Linda Walvoord, PhD, University of Cincinnati

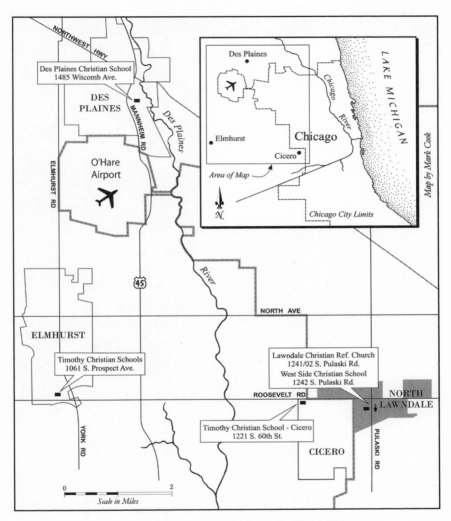

Christian Schools on Chicago's West Side

# Contents

# Acknowledgments

Going on four years ago, Duane VanderBrug asked me if I would be willing to put together a history of the struggle that took place in the Christian Reformed Church over the attempt by black parents in the Chicago area to enroll their children in Timothy Christian School. I knew a bit about Timothy because I had helped write *Flourishing in the Land*, a history of Christian Reformed Home Missions which had a short section put together by my coauthor, Scott Hoezee, about the controversy involving the Christian elementary school in the city of Cicero. Also, as a former newspaper religion editor and news writer for the CRC, I was familiar with aspects of this controversy. But I did not know a great deal about the specifics and, if I thought about it at all, I did not think this one incident that occurred in the 1960s would warrant a book. When Duane asked me to write the story, I thought it might require a couple of months of research to gather thirty or so pages to satisfy his request.

Duane arranged for a few people to meet with me to talk about it, and he asked them to bring in some of their related documents. We talked for a couple of hours, and I took notes. But even as I wrote down some of their remembrances, and then especially as I started going through the volume of material they had dropped off, I began to suspect that I had stepped into a bigger project than I had imagined. To say I got involved slowly, and even with some reluctance, is an understatement. I simply had no idea what an important story this was, how the full story had not been told, and what a far-reaching impact the story would have in the years that followed the resolution of the struggle and even continuing today in the CRC. I began to realize this was a story about racism, when it lives in our hearts and plays out in our everyday lives. It did not take long to realize that the issue involved at Timothy was a much larger issue, and to write about it fully and honestly was going to take more than a couple months of research and thirty or so pages.

The deeper I got into the story, the more complex it became and the more it seemed necessary to make sure I nailed down, as best I was able, every aspect of it. People's lives were involved here; deep emotions and convictions were at work. No one person led the charge in the Timothy conflict. But as I delved into the story, I did find some heroes; they were generally quiet, dedicated people (such as Duane VanderBrug), who lived lives of faith, often behind the scenes, doing their best to guide the situation in what they saw as the right direction. You can read about these people, peppered throughout the book and how they committed themselves to a fight that arose for them out of deeply held Christian convictions.

You can also get an idea of the overriding import of the Timothy story by reading the prologue by Roger Van Harn, a retired CRC pastor and one of those who was there on that first day when I interviewed people. Roger has played a key role in helping to put the manuscript in a publishable form. And there is also the postscript by Joe Ritchie, who now works for the *New York Times*, who grew up in West Lawndale, the area from which many of the parents seeking to enroll their children in Timothy had their homes. In addition, his parents were leaders in the struggle, a struggle that mirrored the overall fight for civil rights that came alive across the United States in the 1960s. To both Van Harn and Joe Richie, I am very grateful for their willingness to offer their thoughts and opinions on a matter that ended up, as readers will see, deeply dividing the CRC and yet also setting it on a new and much healthier and more hopeful path that is yet today working for racial reconciliation.

I am grateful to many other people as well, chief among them is Duane VanderBrug, not only for bringing the idea of writing the story to me but also for keeping after me over the years to write this book. Duane was patient but persistent, never pushy, but always looking ahead to the day when this story, in which he played such an important part, could be told to the wider world. He had the vision and regularly dug through his files to give me material to answer my questions. He is also a careful reader who has worked meticulously to make sure the information in the book is accurate.

As I said, what at first seemed to be a small effort turned into something larger; it required pouring over the mound of material from the people with whom I met on that first day, kept in boxes, files, and dog-eared packets full of yellowing articles which had been underlined and underlined and underlined again. They shared with me papers they had held dear, papers they had gathered over the years which meant a great deal to them because they were part of an important story in which they had had a part.

Throughout the book, these materials are cited in the text where they appear. I have quoted a range of daily newspaper articles, magazine pieces, and stories published in a range of CRC-related publications, such as the *Banner*, the denomination's now monthly magazine, and *Chimes*, the Calvin College student newspaper. Articles also came from the *Reformed Journal*, a magazine that covered a range of issues and matters from a Reformed perspective; *Christian Home and School*, which wrote about the Christian school movement in the CRC; and the *Calvinist Contact* newspaper, a valuable resource for the era in which I was writing. I am also indebted to such books as *Dutch Chicago: A History of the Hollanders in the Windy City*, by historian Robert P. Swierenga, who helped to put the Timothy story, along with some of the politics in the city of Cicero, into perspective. Also valuable was *Shades of White Flight: Evangelical Congregations and Urban Departure*, by social scientist Mark T. Mulder.[1] His book sketches the Timothy conflict and gives an overview of the social forces and different reasons behind the flight of CRC congregations from inner-city Chicago to the outlying suburban areas. Also helpful was *Learning to Count to One*, a book edited by Al Mulder that tells the story of the growing diversity in the CRC and the challenges involved with a change that moved the denomination beyond its predominantly Dutch makeup.

Similarly, I relied extensively on information contained in several annual issues of *Acts of Synod*, which details the decisions made by that year's CRC Synod. These books were invaluable in helping to trace the decisions made by the various Synods, and especially the landmark Synod 1968, in which its delegates deemed racism a sin and—by extension—the decision by the Timothy school board to bar black children from the elementary school as being sinful. The *Acts* also helped me to trace back, with the assistance of a *CRC Viewpoint* booklet, the genesis of statements on racism dating back to the 1950s by the church. The *Acts* also were helpful in determining the way in which the church responded to the Timothy situation after 1968 and running up to

1     New Brunswick, NJ: Rutgers University Press, 2015.

1972 when the matter was concluded after it went before a federal judge in the Chicago area. Along these lines, an interview with and written responses from Case Hoogendoorn, the attorney who defended the Lawndale parents before the judge, were crucial. Helpful as well was the written transcript of the complaint that went to the court before the hearing and especially of the court proceeding itself. I relied as well on issues of the *Timothy Reflector*, the newsletter that the school board published, in telling what went on. An important document put out by the school board, telling its side of why they acted as they did, was *All Things Are Lawful; But Not All Things Are Expedient.*

The minutes from many meetings of Classis Chicago North, the regional church body that addressed the Timothy issue repeatedly, were important, as were the minutes of various CRC offices and agencies such as the Synodical Committee on Racism. With these documents, I was able to trace the changing ways in which the church was working to respond to the Timothy situation and surrounding issues. As you will see, these offices and agencies tended to move one step forward and two steps back as they sought to resolve a matter that, many say, was as much about race relations as it was about a new vision for the church.

Personal letters and correspondence from key people in the story were crucial in helping to fill out the book. Letters written by such leaders as Eugene Bradford, pastor of Ebeneezer CRC in Berwyn, Illinois, gave an inside look at what he—and others whose letters were available—happened to be thinking and feeling as the conflict evolved. Letters to and from the Timothy teachers who quit in protest in 1969 over the school's refusal to admit black students gave an in-depth view of why they did what they did and how they received a great deal of support, along with strong criticism, in the aftermath. Newspaper accounts of the teacher walk-out were also helpful. Again, these articles are cited in the text. Letters and statements issued by Lawndale parents were significant in helping us to see how their optimism in the early days, when they first requested to have their children admitted to Timothy, changed over time. We see how their sentiments moved from optimism and hope, to confusion over why they were being denied, to frustration over the fact that it kept happening, and then to anger and even despair when it seemed their children would never have the chance to go to Timothy. We see how, in fact, they never did have the chance to enroll their children at the school in Cicero. The school, however, eventually did open its doors to black students but only after the school shut down in Cicero and moved to a Chicago suburb, a move chronicled in the court case and in letters, articles, and interviews.

My many interviews were perhaps the most useful source for filling in the full dimensions of this story. To these interviewees, I express heartfelt thanks. All of those I spoke with are identified in the book, including: Duane VanderBrug, Roger Van Harn, Jonathan Bradford, William "Bud" Ipema, Mark Mulder, James Bratt, Paul Kortenhoven, Barbara Campbell, Richard Grevengoed, Peter Huiner, David La Grand, Richard Harms, Esteban Lugo, Karl and Elizabeth Westerhof, Dorothy Ritchie, Mary Post, James Wolff, Reggie Smith, Robert Price, Sheila Brooks, Karen Trout, Clarence "Doc" Taylor, and Gladys Lubben. I am also grateful for a blog post by writer James Schaap who captured the thoughts and feelings of one-time Timothy school board members. They spoke to him about how it was the violently racist nature of Cicero, and the possible threat to black children, that led them to keep denying admission to the children. Schaap is also one of several people who read early versions of this book. Other readers included VanderBrug, Van Harn, Jonathan Bradford, Virginia La Grand, Joe Ritchie, and James Bratt.

Others sources, from US Census Data to the NPR radio show *This American Life*, and from a CRC denominational history to articles in the *Encyclopedia of Chicago*, also offered background and information that kept the book on track and as accurate as possible in all of its elements.

Finally, a visit to West Side Christian School, the school that is a shining example of the hope that emerged from the pain and sorrow that took place over the Timothy conflict, was for me a capstone. The church is located across the street from the former home of Lawndale CRC, the church that was instrumental in pushing to have families seek to have their children admitted to Timothy. With the guidance of Mary Post, the coprincipal, I got to see the school in action. I saw the happy faces of the students representing a spectrum of races in the classrooms and in the hallways. I spoke to those who were involved in the struggle over Timothy and who are active in the school today. The day was inspirational. It showed me a spirit that has not been quenched. It gave me a hands-on, first-hand look at the education being offered to children who may not really know what history had had to occur and unfold before they could be there, and yet who seemed happy that it was available to them.

In the end, I had the chance, as told in chapter thirty-one, detailing the visit, to see the joy of following the commands of Christ being lived out in the place called Lawndale, in a part of Chicago that is still struggling and yet is also alive and in many ways offering a holy light in a time when the entire United States is coming to grips with the reality that, as Jim Wallis, author of the book *Original Sin*, says, "All lives won't matter until black lives matter." All in all, I had the chance in writing this book, with the help of so many others, to tell the tale that is a small part of a very big and eternally significant subject.

# Preface

Rev. Roger E. Van Harn
Pastor Emeritus Christian Reformed Church
(*Archives, Calvin College*)

This is a story about church growth. Not growth in size, but growth in Christ as the apostle Paul described in Galatians 3:28, "There is neither Jew nor Greek, there is neither slave nor free, there is neither male nor female; for you are all one in Christ Jesus." That simple phrase, "in Christ Jesus" was and still is a radical, world-changing word for the worldwide church.

The Triune God's eye is on the world and has been from the beginning. God the Father created the world; the Son redeemed the world, and the Holy Spirit is restoring the world. But when we hear and believe the gospel of Jesus Christ, we follow him in a sinful world with the voices and values of our cultures all around and in us. There is always tension between our faith and our inherited cultures.

In the new beginning, the Pentecost church in Jerusalem, Antioch, and beyond struggled with how Jews and Gentiles could be one in Christ's church. That distinction went back to God's covenant with Abraham in Genesis 12. Even the apostle Peter needed a special vision to accept the gospel for the Gentiles (Acts 10). A more recent experience is when the Christian Reformed Church in North America (CRC) struggled for thirty-five years with whether men and women were permitted to serve together as deacons, elders, and pastors in the church. But perhaps the most painful experience of disunity in our culture and churches is between Anglo and African Americans.

We know from the gospel of Jesus Christ that the unity of all nations and cultures in Christ is both a gift and a calling. The gift is celebrated every time we say the Apostles' Creed. The calling is to practice the unity in Christ in our worship and serving. That is the subject of this story.

It belongs to the genre of storytelling that blossomed in the second half of the twentieth century in North America, where race relations were riddled with conflicts and struggles to reconcile. A notable example is entitled *A Mighty Long Way: My Journey to Justice at Little Rock Central High School*, authored by Carlotta Walls LaNier.[1]

---

[1]    New York: One World Books, 2009.

She was the youngest member (age 14) of the famous Little Rock Nine, black students who were escorted by the National Guard to desegregate the school in Arkansas on September 25, 1957. The resulting abuse and violence against these nine students and their heroic response formed a lifelong bond among them that led to a reunion every decade on that date. The book was published following the fiftieth anniversary by Random Books. Coincidentally, this present story is told by Christopher Meehan fifty years after the race struggle it describes.

Bill Clinton is a native of Arkansas, a former governor of the state, and later president of the United States. He befriended the Nine and attended their thirtieth, fortieth, and fiftieth reunions. He also contributed the foreword for the book that tells their story. His closing words can tell the truth about many stories of race relations among us: *"A Mighty Long Way* will make you ashamed and proud, angry and hopeful, heartsick and happy. Carlotta tells it as it was, a story we all need to know."

The urgency to tell the story of Lawndale Church[2] and Timothy School[3] surfaced following the dedication of the Chicago West Side Christian School in Lawndale on November 21, 2004. At the dedication service, Rev. Duane VanderBrug[4] told the story

---

[2]    Lawndale Christian Reformed Church began as a mission, 1926-27, 1950-, and was organized as a church in 1963. It continues as a thriving church of the CRC. *Yearbook 2014 CRC* (Grand Rapids: CRC Denominational Services, 2014), 211 (henceforth: *Yearbook*).

[3]    Timothy Christian School was founded in 1911. Its building at 14th St. and 59th Ct., Cicero, was erected in 1927. Robert P. Swierenga, *Dutch Chicago: A History of the Hollanders in the Windy City* (Grand Rapids, Eerdmans, 2002), 422-23.

[4]    VanderBrug, Duane Edward. Calvin Theological Seminary, BD, 1960; McCormick Theological Seminary, DMin, 1985; Manhattan CRC, West Harlem, NYC, minister of evangelism, 1960-62; ordained 1962, home missionary, Richton Park, IL, 1962-66; Missionary Lawndale, Chicago, 1966-69, assistant field secretary of Home Missions, 1969-75; director of personnel, Board of Home Missions, Grand Rapids, MI, 1975-91; director, Established Church Development, Grand Rapids, MI, 1991-97; church development specialist and regional director, Eastern USA region, Grand Rapids, MI, 1998-2004; CRC Ministry Plan Implementation Team, Grand Rapids, MI, 1998-2000; Home Missions Conferences coordinator, Grand Rapids, MI, 2000-2003; retired 2003, hospital chaplain, 2004-11; Classis Georgetown of the CRCNA, Classis Renewal and Vision Team facilitator, 2004-16; per author email,

of how and why Lawndale children had been bussed twenty-eight miles to the Des Plaines Christian School[5] in 1967, while he was serving as Lawndale church's pastor. He also explained that when the Des Plaines facilities reached capacity, the bussing continued to the Timothy Christian School campus in Elmhurst in 1972. He then asked those present to stand if they had either rode or driven that school bus. About twenty stood and were celebrated with an enthusiastic ovation. When some of the school staff and teachers said that they had not heard that part of the story before, Rev. Bud Ipema[6] challenged Duane to do what President Clinton had said about Carlotta's Little Rock story: "Tell it as it was, a story we all need to hear." That was the beginning of the story that is now before us.

As the story unfolds, it will become evident that the telling of it is a *communal* effort. The many people who lived the story were consulted and contributed the resources. It will also become clear that the "growing pains" named in the title afflicted the many "sides" that can be counted in the many-sided struggle. There was enough pain all around to urge the community to pray and work for healing and growth in the one Body of Christ.

The story of Lawndale Church and Timothy School belongs to the larger story of Little Rock Central High School and the National Guard. These stories belong to the largest story of sin and grace that began in the Garden of Eden when Adam and Eve

Feb. 2, 2017 and *Historical Directory of the Christian Reformed Church*, comp. and ed., Richard H. Harms (Grand Rapids: Historical Committee of the Christian Reformed Church in North America, 2004), 347 (henceforth, *Historical Directory*), *Yearbook 2014*, 639.

5    See Swierenga, *Dutch Chicago*, 282, 432, 442.

6    Ipema, William (Bud). Calvin Theological Seminary, BD, 1969, ordained 1975, faculty, North Park Seminary, Oak Lawn, IL, 1975-80; director of Multi-Racial Leadership Development, Synodical Committee on Race Relations, Oak Park, IL, 1980-86; SCORR, Oak Park, IL, 1986-87, president, Mid-America Leadership Foundation, Chicago, IL, 1987-2001; vice president, Council of Leadership Foundations, Chicago, IL, 2001-, Timothy Institute, Grand Rapids, MI, 2007-, retired 2011. *Historical Directory*, 240; *Yearbook 2014*, 581-82.

went into hiding from God in their sin, and God sought them out and asked, "Where are you?" (Genesis 3:9). Grace prevailed. In the fullness of time, after having lunch with a sinner named Zacchaeus, Jesus announced, "For the Son of Man came to seek and to save the lost" (Luke 19:10).

Grace prevails

# Prologue

# Out of Cicero

Rev. Peter B. Huiner (*photo ca. 1964*)
Pastor, Lawndale Christian
Reformed Church,
February 1962 to January 1966
(*Archives, Calvin College*)

"Nathanael said, 'Can anything good come out of Nazareth?'
Philip said to him, 'Come and see.'" John 1:46

The town of Cicero is Chicago's first suburb on its western border. Built mainly in the 1930s, it has always been a working-class community. Brick bungalows and two-flat residences stand only a few feet from each other. They are bordered by ten-foot front lawns and small, fenced-in backyards. People of means occupied houses on the corner of the block, but even these homes were modest. Cicero had no mansions.

In the mid-twentieth century, this community was made up of second-generation immigrant families, primarily Dutch, Italian, and Bohemian. Many of them had formerly lived in the city, but they were now moving up the economic ladder and buying their first home in the suburbs. Others settled in the town because of "white flight." African Americans had moved into Chicago's west side, and the old residents fled. Red-lining realtors warned them that their property values would plummet unless they immediately sold their homes and moved. Cicero had the reputation of being a safe refuge, since it was known to be completely white.

Cicero was my home; my roots are there. I grew up in a lovely, secure world. Our family lived on the same block on Sixty-First Avenue for my entire childhood. We knew most of the people in our neighborhood. At least half of them were Dutch. The westward migration of the Dutch immigrant community of Chicago now formed the majority population of Cicero's north end. Most of the important places in our childhood were close by. We walked to school, to the grocery store, and to the homes of our relatives. Most of the people we knew were associated with the garbage-hauling or cartage business. Our doctors and dentists were Dutch. We put our Christmas Club savings in the Dutch-owned savings bank. We patronized Rusthoven's and Van Dyke's dry goods store. We paid our premiums to the Dutch Self Help Insurance Company. When someone died, the service was held at Mulder's, with burial in the Dutch section of Forest Home Cemetery.

Our secure community was deeply religious. Anchoring the whole lives of the second- and third-generation immigrants was the trinity of "Kingdom causes"—the church, the Christian school, and missionary work. Two Christian Reformed churches, First Cicero and Warren Park, were built a few blocks from each other. A third one, Ebenezer, stood on the border between Cicero and Berwyn, and a fourth congregation was established in nearby Oak Park.

Morning and evening services plus Sunday school took our family to church for at least five hours every Sunday. Our relatives all went to the same church, and we gathered at each other's homes after the services. We went back to church during the week for catechism classes. Mother went to Ruth Circle for fellowship and to plan the annual Silver Tea and the rummage sale. Dad was always on the consistory as deacon or elder. Church was central to life.

The second foundation of the community was the Christian school. By Reformed belief, baptized children were members of the "Covenant of Grace." Parents were obligated to provide them with a faith-based education. While organizationally separate from each other, the school and the church were inseparably wedded. We had special offerings in church for Timothy Christian School and Chicago Christian High, and we prayed in church for the success of school fund drives. Timothy Christian's eighth-grade graduation was held at First Cicero. On Reformation Day, the entire student body walked a block to Warren Park for a special rally. Notices of school activities filled the church bulletins.

Christian education was a primary focus of the Huiners. My immigrant grandfather was a founding father of the first Christian school on Chicago's west side. According to family lore, he had chosen the school's name—Ebenezer (Hitherto hath the Lord helped us). My parents lived and breathed Christian education. Not surprisingly, Dad served on the Timothy board

Bernard Huiner
(*courtesy Tona Huiner*)

for many years. As board president, he handed me my Bible at my eighth-grade graduation. He championed the building of the new Timothy Christian High School across from First Cicero Church. My younger brother was in the first graduating class there. Mother devoted herself to Friendship Club's school fundraising. The school's teachers were frequent dinner guests in our home. Cicero was my home, and Timothy School was my heritage. It was, in many ways, a good and godly place.

At the same time, life in Cicero was complicated, even within the sheltered Dutch community. The organized crime syndicate controlled local politics and the police force. Everyone knew it. We mainly just lived with it. As children, we even went Halloween trick-or-treating at the home of Al Capone's brother. The garbage men and truckers among the church members were doing business in Chicago. That meant that they were forced to make moral compromises in dealing with the syndicate. Cicero produced cynicism and fear along with security and piety.

Racism was deeply embedded in the Cicero mentality. It was not limited to our town, of course, but it was an inevitable price of living in our town. We prided ourselves on our all-white population. Black people might work in Cicero, but they could never live there. Any person of color seen on the street after six o'clock in the evening was likely to be stopped by the police. A black family once tried to move into town, and Cicero responded. The building was torched, and the National Guard stood watch a block from our home. That family wisely decided to live elsewhere.

Our home and school shared the racism of our community. At Timothy School, we were taught that the position of "Negroes" in society was due to the "Curse of Ham."[1] Many Dutch families were fearful because they had lost money when they felt they were forced to sell their old homes. They blamed it on the "colored." My father employed black workers, but there were no social relations with them. He could tell racial jokes, in dialect. He never missed listening to the "Amos and Andy Show." One year we children applied burnt cork to our faces for Halloween and went out as minstrels. When we got together with friends, we bandied about the "n-word" freely, along with several other even more offensive names. Racism and fear were part of what it meant to live in Cicero. Could anything good come out of Cicero?

Out of Cicero—working-class, city-fled, defensive, insular, racist Cicero—came the movement of the Holy Spirit. The devout Dutch were a mission-minded people. Nigerian pioneer missionary Tena Huizenga was supported by First Cicero, and her furlough visits were hailed and revered. Women's Missionary Union meetings featured all-day programs of missionary speakers. Our church aired a weekly gospel program on the local radio station. Teams of Light Bearer Volunteers visited County Hospital to sing hymns and distribute tracts. The Helping Hand Mission was a locally sponsored rescue mission on the Madison Street skid row.

---

[1]   Gen. 9:25.

Lawndale Church in the 1967 snowstorm which dropped 23.5 inches in twenty-four hours, giving rise to looting and burning (*courtesy Duane VanderBrug*)

Nathanael Institute was an evangelistic outreach to the Jewish community. It occupied a solidly built, well-equipped facility in the Lawndale community on Chicago's west side. The building included a small chapel, a gymnasium, a medical clinic, and a variety of meeting rooms. During the 1950s, the Jewish population migrated to the city's north side, and Nathanael Institute went with them. The Jewish residents were replaced by the continuing westward movement of African Americans, who were now living all the way to the Cicero boundary line. Classis Chicago North decided to put the well-built, strategically located building to a new use. By a miracle of grace, it was renamed "Lawndale Gospel Chapel." Clarence Buist, a dedicated Reformed Bible Institute graduate, became the evangelist. Enthusiastic volunteers were recruited from the Cicero churches, notably from Warren Park. They taught Sunday school, led Bible classes, and ran youth programs. Soon there were professions of faith and baptisms. Since Lawndale was an unorganized mission, the memberships were registered at Warren Park. The Christian

Reformed Church in Cicero now included black members! Who could have predicted it?

Due to the growth of the Lawndale ministry, the Home Missions Committee of Classis decided to call an ordained pastor to lead the congregation. They searched for a candidate who had some experience in inner-city ministry and who would be sensitive to the ethos of Cicero, including its racial tensions. At that time, the denomination's only African American congregation was New York's Mid-Harlem Community Parish/Manhattan Church. I had been the first Calvin Theological Seminary student to experience an internship year in Harlem . . . and I was from Cicero. Even before my graduation or being declared a candidate for ministry, I had received a visit. In the fall of 1961, the Revs. Fred Van Houten and Earl Marlink, representing the Classical committee, came to Grand Rapids to recruit me for the Lawndale job. I accepted the offer and began work the following February. I was finally ordained at Warren Park Church in September 1962. Many of Lawndale's black members attended the Cicero service and were warmly welcomed. Within two years, the congregation was formally organized as Lawndale Christian Reformed Church. Its elders took their seats at Classis. The congregation outgrew their chapel and began to worship in the gymnasium. Summer programs were led by denominational youth teams. I was invited to preach and tell the Lawndale story at local churches, the Women's Missionary Union, and chapel services in the Timothy Christian High School.

I have been described as a "social activist" in my ministry. In reality, my ministry at Lawndale was very traditional. The church had two Sunday services, both with a sermon and with one fulfilling the rule of Heidelberg Catechism themes. I led a weekly Ladies' Bible Class. I organized and directed an adult choir. Classes were held to prepare people for profession of faith and baptism. We held Vacation Bible School and Backyard Bible Story

Lawndale at worship, led by Pastor Duane VanderBrug
(*courtesy Duane Vanderbrug*)

Time in the summer. I worked to educate the new congregation
in the history and polity of the Christian Reformed Church. And,
of course, I preached and taught the Reformed understanding of
Christianity, including the Covenant of Grace. True to my family
heritage, I regularly preached on the need for Christian schools.
That idea took a while to catch on at Lawndale church, since these
schools are costly, and many people had limited financial means.
Also, attending a Christian school would involve transportation
problems, since Timothy, the nearest school, was about three
miles away. Church members were not initially interested.

I continued to champion Christian schools for another
reason. The quality of public education in Chicago at that time
was appalling. I heard first-hand reports on the local schools
from a teacher in our congregation, from parents, and neighbors.
I began to try to convince our parents to send their covenant
children to nearby Timothy. As a Cicero native, whose parents still
lived there, I understood the challenge. I was aware that enrolling
black children in a school in racially charged Cicero would be
problematic and controversial. At the same time, I assured our

parents that the school could not turn away children who were members of the Christian Reformed Church. They had, after all, been sought out, welcomed, and supported by the churches right in the Timothy neighborhood.

Conversations began with the Timothy school board in the spring of 1965. I kept no record of these conversations. I do, however, remember that we were urged by the board not to proceed with our plans to enroll children that fall. We were warned that such a move could provoke violent resistance in Cicero. It could potentially endanger the school children. Our Lawndale parents, however, were prepared to take that risk. They officially informed the board of their intention to enroll their children in September. The board responded that the children would not be admitted.

The lines were now drawn. Fierce debate began within the wider Christian Reformed community. I began to receive hostile letters and threatening phone calls, including several death threats. Some of these were anonymous. Most of them came from church members and school board members. I had known these people from my youth, friends of my parents, my old Cicero neighbors.

It soon became clear to me that my effectiveness as Lawndale's pastor had become compromised. I was being held personally responsible for trying to "force integration" at Timothy. The Civil Rights Movement was changing the country, and it was changing me. What had begun out of concern for the children of our parish and a conviction that these children had a right to Christian education had become a broader issue: confronting racism in the community and the denomination of my birth. A Cicero man was now seen as a traitor to his own people. It was time for me to move on. We left Lawndale the following January.

The ensuing denominational controversy has been described as "tragic." In some sense that is no doubt true. I had believed, perhaps naively, that the good godly Dutch of Cicero, who worked and sacrificed for mission, would ultimately stand up to Cicero's racism. Faith would overcome fear. I was right in believing that. It took years to develop, but it did happen. A joyful reunion of Timothy's African American alumni was a featured part of Timothy's recent centennial celebration.

Can anything good come out of Cicero? Come and see.

# CHAPTER 1

# The First Day of School

Sheila Brooks stepped off the old International school bus at 8:45 a.m., the day after Labor Day, September 1967, and walked, along with nearly twenty other students from Lawndale Christian Reformed Church, into the Des Plaines Christian School.

She was scared; all of them were scared on that warm and sunny morning. Sheila had no idea how she would be treated in this white school, thirty miles from their urban Chicago neighborhood. For that matter, she was not entirely sure why they had to go there. Her parents told her it was so she could get a better education than she was receiving at the elementary school in Lawndale where kids were rowdy, and classrooms were so overcrowded that students were on half days. At the same time, she had heard hints about problems her parents and other parents were having trying to enroll the children in a Christian school in a community much closer to home, but it was not until years later that she understood that conflict.

Lawndale children and their parents in Des Plaines, Illinois
(*courtesy Duane VanderBrug*)

"I remember walking into the new school, and my mom had told me to be on my best behavior," said Brooks, who in 2016 was an elder at Lawndale CRC. "I wasn't sure how they would accept us in the Des Plaines school. But we were introduced to our new classmates, and it was pretty cool. I felt accepted right away, even if they put me back into fifth grade because I wasn't really prepared to do the work of sixth."

In 1965 Brooks' parents, as well as other parents at Lawndale CRC, had applied to send their baptized children to Timothy Christian School, located in Cicero, about three miles from their church. Going there would have been much easier, but the school board at Timothy refused to admit the students—the parents were convinced—because of their race. The school board, on the other hand, believed it would be too dangerous for them to attend the school in racist Cicero.

For Sheila, one of the biggest problems with going to Des Plaines was that, when standing with her school bag at the bus stop, her friends would single her out and make fun of her, wondering aloud why she was waiting for that special bus. "I learned to deal with it," she said.

Lynn Taylor, another Des Plaines student, said in a paper she later wrote about her experience at Des Plaines that she had a little harder time adjusting. "I had a grudge [when she first went there]. Education was a mere stage I had to go through because I thought the whites would never let us prove what we knew," she said. But at the Des Plaines Christian School, her attitude slowly improved. "Des Plaines has helped me to change my thoughts through the grace of God," she wrote. "And I thank him for letting me be here."

Sheila Brooks and Lynn Taylor were part of a story that has echoed throughout the years, full of disturbing lessons and significant developments for the Christian Reformed Church and for the broader church as well. Sheila and Lynn may not have realized they were in the vanguard of a movement characterized by parents seeking to get a Christian education at the school three miles away for their children. But they were playing a role in what turned out to be an important stage in defining the way the CRC denomination has addressed race relations down through the decades. They were part of what proved to be a crucial turning point for the church—a turning point which brought the words in the Bible into sharp focus in a real-life situation.

"The Christian Reformed Church and its individual members are faced with one of the most significant crisis of its history," attorney Case Hoogendoorn would write in a 1971 memo before he filed a federal lawsuit in this matter. "The Timothy-Lawndale situation presents the problem of attempting to apply abstract biblical principles in a concrete historical setting."

Before jumping into the story, we will look at the historical setting that Hoogendoorn mentioned; at the most influential voices in the matter, both up front and behind the scenes; and how the decade in which the clash occurred irrevocably shaped these events.

Artist's rendering of Timothy Christian Elementary School, built in 1927, on Fourteenth Street and Fiftieth Avenue, in Cicero, Illinois (*Archives, Calvin College*)

# CHAPTER 2

# Leading the Charge

In the vanguard of the cause of trying to integrate Timothy Christian School was a group of Christian Reformed pastors. Others, such as attorney Case Hoogendoorn, were also important advocates. But it was the pastors, as ministry leaders, who had the highest profile. Unlike today, there were no black CRC minsters in Chicago to take up the struggle, although several were growing up—one right in Lawndale—and would eventually assume leadership roles in the church. But in the 1960s, as the Timothy battle began, it was white ministers such as Peter Huiner,[1] Duane VanderBrug, Eugene Bradford, James La Grand, Jacob Boonstra, and Joel Nederhood who stepped into the fray and sought for the sake of the gospel to obtain a rightful place for black students.

---

[1]  Huiner, Peter Bruce, Calvin Theological Seminary, BD, 1960; ordained 1962; Manhattan, New York, NY, 1959-60; Home Missionary, Lawndale, IL, 1962-66; Grace, Grand Rapids, MI, 1966-69; Episcopal Church, 1970; *Historical Directory*, 236.

As we shall see, being part of this struggle was a straightforward decision for these pastors. They did not wonder whether their participation was right. In the end, joining this fight was natural and became a highlight of their ministry. Huiner and VanderBrug served as the first pastors of Lawndale CRC and played key roles in helping Lawndale parents in their effort to have their children attend Timothy. La Grand[2] was pastor of Garfield CRC and remained an outspoken advocate for opening the doors of Timothy to black youngsters.

Boonstra[3] was pastor of First CRC in Cicero, directly across the street from Timothy. He attended many meetings about this issue during this time, sometimes to the chagrin of his own parishioners, and he once found himself at odds with a white supremacist group that did not like what he was saying (see chapter 26). Overall, Boonstra, like many others, said the battle over admitting black students turned into a critical moment in his ministry and for the CRC itself. Boonstra saw the fight as reflecting a deeper rift in society at large and the attempt by people of good will to fix it. It was a turbulent time for many people, himself included, but he was grateful to have been part of it.

Eugene Bradford[4] was pastor of Ebenezer CRC in Berwyn, the church that pushed hard for the CRC Synod 1968 to call

---

[2]    La Grand, James, Jr., Calvin Theological Seminary, ThM. 1975; ordained 1969, Garfield, Chicago, IL, 1969-74; leave, 1974-75; Centennial Missions Scholarship, 1975-76; All Nations, Halifax, NS, 1977-87; leave, 1987-88; eligible for call, 1988-91; teacher, Chicago Metropolitan Center, Chicago, IL, 1991-92; faculty, Lutheran School of Theology, Chicago, IL, 1993; Beacon Light, Gary, IN, 1993-; retired 2006; *Historical Directory*, 265 and *Yearbook 2014*, 597.

[3]    Boonstra, Jacob Paul, Calvin Theological Seminary, BD, 1950; ThB, 1953; ordained 1953; Cascade, MI, 1953-57; Twelfth Street, Grand Rapids, MI, 1957-63; First, Cicero, IL, 1963-68; Hillcrest, Denver, CO, 1968-77; Plainfield, Rockford, MI, 1977-86; Tracy, IA, 1986-92; retired, 1992; *Historical Directory*, 157.

[4]    Bradford, Dallas Eugene, Westminster Theological Seminary, ThD, 1941; ordained, 1941; Independent: Faith Presbyterian, Fawn Grove, PA, 1941-44; OPC, Calvary, Philadelphia, PA, 1944-51; CRC, Flint, MI, 1951-54; Third, Paterson, NJ, 1954-61; associate pastor, Third, Paterson; and executive secretary of Westminster Theological Seminary, 1961-63; Ebenezer, Berwyn, IL, 1963-69; Franklyn Lakes, NJ, 1969-74; Maple Ave., Holland, MI, 1974-80; retired, 1980; *Historical Directory*, 162.

Rev. Joel Nederhood
(*Archives, Calvin College*)

the actions of the Timothy school board sinful. Because of his involvement in the issue, he and his family were subjected to hateful criticism and were once threatened by a woman who called their home, warning them that someone was going to shoot a gun through their window. Still, despite the threats, in a letter, Bradford wrote: "As I look back, I surely conclude the Timothy-Lawndale matter was the highlight of my sixty years in ministry. I had no choice; the Lord gave me the vision and the strength and hope."

For Nederhood,[5] the CRC's radio preacher for the *Back to God Hour*, the Timothy struggle was important in many ways. The issue touched his conscience. This was no small matter. It had a much broader context, reminding him of the need to promote Christ's good news to all people. In an article in the *Banner*, the CRC's periodical, Nederhood said he considered the battle as an

---

[5] Nederhood, Joel Homan, Calvin Theological Seminary, BD, 1957; Vrije Universiteit, Amsterdam, ThD, 1960; ordained, 1960; radio minister, *Back to God Hour*, Palos Heights, IL, 1960-86; director of ministries, *Back to God Hour*, 1986-96; retired, 1996; *Historical Directory*, 285.

important effort to address the "institutionalized racism that grows everywhere on the soil of our continent." The Timothy situation, he wrote, was not an isolated incident; he charged the CRC with having "demonstrated more often than not that it is unable to receive as equals those of another race." When this happens, he went on, in any church, racism "renders a Church structurally incapable of demonstrating the fellowship that must arise when people who love the Lord Jesus find themselves bound together in a unity that makes all ordinary human differences secondary, if not inconsequential."

Although many pastors displayed absolute courage in pressing forward with the demands of their faith, to be clear, it was the Lawndale parents, who doggedly pursued enrolling their children in a Christian school in the midst of a racially charged situation, under threat of violence, intimidation, and excuses, that personified heroism. And these parents, with the importunity of the persistent neighbor,[6] caused the doors of the "covenant community" to be opened and justice granted.

The Lawndale parents and the CRC pastors fighting for racial justice believed that Christ meant it when he said that love was the greatest commandment and that we should love others, meaning *all* others, as we love ourselves. Fighting for this cause, however, took a toll on some of those on the frontlines. In some cases, pastors' careers were stymied; in others, health problems cropped up. But they took a stand, shining light on evil. Like a chorus of modern-day prophets, they urged their church and community to confront one of the most persistent problems of our time and to begin a long journey, much fraught with peril.

---

[6]    Luke 11:5-10.

# CHAPTER 3

# An Enduring Impact

The CRC's efforts in urban ministry date back to the 1960s, to churches such as Manhattan CRC in West Harlem, New York City, and to Lawndale in Chicago, where the ministers and church members sought to live out the full gospel in a quickly changing urban setting. As he looked back, Karl Westerhof said it was an exciting time of fresh possibilities for him to serve as an interim pastor at Lawndale in the late sixties.

During this time, the people at the new church in Lawndale were on fire for their faith and living out the gospel in different ways, among them, seeking to enroll their children in the nearby Christian school. Also, writing in the *Banner*, Westerhof said these years made up a hopeful era, for himself and for others at Lawndale and elsewhere, in which many "voices are beginning to cry in loud tones that the work of God must be carried out in the cities. And it is an exciting thing to see Christ at work."

Karl Westerhof
(*courtesy John Steigenga*)

Exciting, to be sure, but it had its consequences. As we shall see, the struggle between Lawndale and Timothy was a conflict that divided the church and yet also brought it, or at least certain factions of it, together in important ways. "This was a painful time and situation, but I believe that God made good to come of it, for people of color and for the CRC," said Barbara Campbell Otten, who grew up in Lawndale CRC and later ran a ground-breaking education ministry at the church. Although she was too old at the time for her parents to enroll her in the Timothy Christian Elementary School, she was very familiar with the attempt by members of the church for their children to receive a Christian education.

Barbara later attended the Timothy Christian High School located outside Chicago in Elmhurst for her senior year and then went on to graduate with a teaching degree from Calvin College. In 1973 she returned to serve as director of religious education and community programming at Lawndale. Among other things, she helped to oversee the Sunday school and the outreach to seniors, developed education curricula tailored directly to children in the neighborhood, and coordinated summer programs for youth.

Barbara Campbell Otten, 1964
(*courtesy Huiners*)

In the process, her "ministry was generally considered to be of such excellent caliber that it served as a model for other inner-city mission efforts," wrote Scott Hoezee, in the history of home missions, titled *Flourishing in the Land.*

Growing up in the area, attending Calvin, and then working in ministry at Lawndale, gave Barbara an especially clear view of what the struggle over Timothy meant. "What happened between Timothy and Lawndale brought the issue of racism to people's minds in the CRC," said Campbell Otten. "It took time, but confronting racism at Timothy seems to me to be an example

Rev. Scott Hoezee
(*Archives, Calvin College*)

Pulaski Road looking northwest from Lawndale Church
(*courtesy John Steigenga*)

Pulaski Road looking southwest from Lawndale Church
(*courtesy John Steigenga*)

of how this country—and the CRC—has been able to make slow progress."

Slow progress, to be sure, given that race relations in America in 2016 remain problematic at best. But the CRC did address this conflict, and this story is a story of how a small church, and especially some of is pastors, tried to tackle a tough, nearly overwhelming issue, and in some ways succeeded and in other ways fell short. In the process, though, this is a story of strength and courage, not only of the pastors but also, notably, of the parents who pushed hard for integration and persisted, even though they were denied time after time. It is also tale of how one church faced its own sin and racism and, as Campbell Otten said, began to make changes in its individual ministries and institutions.

# CHAPTER 4

# The Christian Reformed Church
# Was Not Immune

Without a doubt, the fact that the school controversy took place during the turbulent 1960s was critical. That decade, a time of great social upheaval in the United States, made the struggle what it was; the era and the experience were synonymous and inextricably linked.

During the 1960s, drugs and rock and roll were challenging the status quo; morals were loosening. Every minority culture began looking to its own history, heritage, and power in a variety of liberation movements, which often led traditional authority figures and institutions to be fearful and anxious. The Vietnam War drew widespread protests, further dividing society and culture, and ultimately led to the downfall, many say, of President Lyndon Johnson.

Urban riots took place throughout the country, including Chicago, particularly in Lawndale where much of the area

National Guard on Sixteenth Street as seen through the back
window of VanderBrug's car (*courtesy Duane VanderBrug*)

went up in flames, and whole streets were destroyed following
the assassination on April 4, 1968, of Rev. Martin Luther King
Jr. Chicago was also the place where, in the summer of 1968,
blood ran in the streets outside the 1968 Democratic National
Convention when anti-Vietnam War protestors went head to
head with Chicago police officers clad in royal blue helmets and
riot gear.

This was also the period in which the US Congress finally
approved, and President Johnson signed, the 1964 Civil Rights
Act, which outlawed discrimination in hiring, promoting, and
firing workers. This was followed in 1965 by the passage and
signing of the Voting Rights Act, aimed at overcoming legal
barriers at the state and local levels which prevented African
Americans from exercising their right to vote. In addition, during
this tumultuous era, bus boycotts and KKK rallies shattered the
peace. In Selma, Alabama, "Bloody Sunday" took place on March
7, 1965, when police on horseback, wielding clubs, clashed on the
Edmund Pettus Bridge with nonviolent, voting-rights workers.
For those who did not live through this period, it might be hard
to picture what this was like. For society at large, things were in
constant transition. Tradition was besieged on nearly every front.

View from VanderBrug's kitchen window on Cullerton St., across three junk-filled lots next to Sixteenth Street where businesses were being burned out, 1968 (*courtesy Duane VanderBrug*)

And focusing in more sharply, we see that the CRC was not immune. "The flood of changes in values, lifestyles, and social interactions precipitated in the 1960s profoundly affected the CRC. Tidier patterns of church life gave way to a rising disenchantment and disagreement over how believers should respond to the social chaos around them," according to a denominational history. For instance, says the history, the role of women in church leadership "became a hotly contested conflict during the sixties. Changing roles for women in the larger society forced the CRC to ask whether women should be allowed to serve in ecclesiastical office."

During this time, the issue of race also loomed large in various quarters of the CRC, but it was especially in Chicago that the CRC had its own cauldron of trouble brewing at Timothy.

Mark T. Mulder
*(courtesy Mark Mulder)*

This is where the CRC had to cross its own Edmund Pettus Bridge. The situation in West Chicago never approached the level that it did in Alabama, but the same issues—the same racism—were in play. This is where, on a smaller scale, four teachers at Timothy walked out to protest the racism in that school. On the day they quit, up to fifty CRC members and supporters walked through the neighborhood, praying and singing, joining in solidarity with the teachers.

The Lawndale and Timothy controversy became ground zero in the sixties in the fight for equal rights and shone an unfavorable light on the ways in which the CRC was struggling to get beyond its Dutch heritage.

"As African Americans arrived in CRC community neighborhoods in Chicago on the wings of the Great Migration, one particular school (Timothy) became a battleground that would vividly illustrate the limitation of insular social circles (in the CRC)," writes Mark Mulder, a Calvin College sociologist, in his book *White Flight*.[1]

[1]     *Shades of White Flight: Evangelical Congregations and Urban Departure* (New Brunswick, NJ: Rutgers University Press, 2015), 45.

Traditional, white CRC members at Timothy fought to keep black children out of the school, largely because, school board members said, of the racist and reactionary nature of the city of Cicero. But, Mulder argues, it was also because the children were not part of the CRC's "closed system," meaning a system run and populated by mainly white, Dutch immigrants and their families. For these people, good Christian education in largely CRC-supported schools among their own was spiritually crucial, if not socially imperative. Even though the denomination itself spoke forcefully, especially in 1968, decrying the actions of the school board at Timothy, the localized way in which the CRC is governed left all the power for decision making in the hands of Cicero school officials. The Christian schools are independent of the CRC, even though most of those on the Timothy board were members of the CRC.

The confrontation between the African American parents and the twelve-member Timothy school board "left an ugly legacy in the area for the CRC," writes Mulder. "It became an emblematic episode of the failures of a closed community. Beyond that, it clearly demonstrated the local authority that dominated the CRC."

Today, the Timothy Christian Elementary School has been moved and is located on a campus with the high school twenty-two miles to the west in Elmhurst.[2] Many say it is an exemplar of racial integration. But back then, the elementary and junior high schools remained in Cicero. Deep emotions divided decent people with good intentions in the CRC over the Timothy issue. Ultimately it went before Synod 1968, and in 1972, it landed in federal court. "The story of the Timothy school is a good case study in the issue of race relations in the CRC," per James Bratt, professor of history at Calvin College. "It happened at the peak of the moment of the civil rights movement in 1960s America,

[2]    1061 S. Prospect Ave., Elmhurst, IL.

James Bratt
(*Archives, Calvin College*)

showing how that reverberated across northern as well as southern states."

The story also reflects the tension in the value system of CRC members, tension that remains yet today, said Bratt. On the one hand, CRC commitment to Christian schools, such as Timothy, demonstrated a desire to be faithful to the gospel in all areas of life, exemplifying the Reformed world-life view, which says, "no square inch" of creation—including education—is outside of the sovereignty of God and the mission of his people. "CRC members' commitment to the Covenant shows the importance of Christian solidarity for one another and the church across the generations and geographic distance," said Bratt. "Yet the Timothy case shows that solidarity stopping at the boundaries of race."

Other values of CRC life are also exemplified here, says Bratt, such as "the importance of being respectably middle-class, of property values, and of conforming to prevailing American values, particularly on matters of race." The Timothy school board's decisions fit right in with many of these values by "taking a classic American way out: moving to the suburbs. Ironically,

Chicago West Side Christian School today
(*courtesy Mary Post*)

the people who posed a problem for them started up a Christian school in the area that Timothy left behind, faithful to the historic vision of the CRC."

Bratt was referring to Chicago West Side Christian School,[3] a multicultural elementary school of some 190 students, now located in a building across from the former Lawndale church building. It is a beacon of reconciliation that emerged from the battle over Timothy.

---

[3]    1240 S. Pulaski Road, Chicago, IL.

# CHAPTER 5

# The Fight Begins

Lawndale CRC was started in the late 1940s as a chapel in a Chicago storefront in a neighborhood on the corner of Thirteenth Street and Karlov Avenue. At that time, the CRC established chapels in urban areas such as Lawndale, instead of planting "emerging churches" as it does today. Generally, the hope was these chapels would eventually grow and become churches. At the same time, however, there was another, less obvious, reason for the founding of these chapels. In *Learning to Count to One: The Joy and Pain of Becoming a Multiracial Church*, edited by Al Mulder (2006), there is this quote from an observer of the chapel movement that illustrates this agenda: "The intent of the chapel strategy was simply to create safe space for non-Dutch folks to encounter the gospel. A side benefit was that chapels also relieved Dutch folks' uneasiness with 'others' who were not familiar with CRC tradition and culture."[1]

---

[1]    Grand Rapids, MI: Faith Alive (2006), 94.

Rev. Al Mulder
(*Archives, Calvin College*)

Initially, Lawndale Chapel was home mostly to poor, southern whites who had come north to work in one of the factories, such as International Harvester, General Electric, or the sprawling Sears Roebuck headquarters, factories which were plentiful and within easy walking distance. Then as the whites began to prosper and move out in the years following World War II, blacks, many of them from the Mississippi Delta, moved in and began worshipping at the chapel. Although the ministry at the chapel started slowly, it picked up and eventually flourished when, under the leadership of lay evangelist Clarence Buist,[2] the chapel moved into the former Nathaniel Institute in the 1950s.

Built in 1928, this institute was a sturdy, two-story building, which for many years had housed the CRC's outreach to Jewish people who by then were leaving the area and moving to the city's north side. The building included a small chapel, a gymnasium, a medical clinic, and a variety of meeting rooms. Ministry at the institute took place mostly to Eastern European Jews who had

---

[2]    Buist was a "Full-time Lay Missionary in the Field of Evangelism" and is listed as such in the *Yearbook 1963 of the Christian Reformed Church*, serving the Lawndale Chapel from 1953-63, p. 329. *Historical Directory*, 21.

Evangelist Clarence Buist and
Lawndale church members
(*courtesy, Tona Huiner*)

filled the neighborhoods and owned local businesses for many years. Even today, many buildings that once housed Jewish synagogues and community centers are visible on a tour of Lawndale. These structures—many still decorated with a Star of David—reflect the strong influence this group once had on the area.

Located at 1241 South Pulaski Road, a major north-south street near Roosevelt Road, the institute stood in a neighborhood of larger, older, two-flat, stone-front homes, built shoulder to shoulder on streets running off the business districts. The houses were made of brick to protect against fire. People sought these kinds of homes following the Great Chicago Fire that rampaged for three days, killing some three hundred people and destroying much of the city in October 1871.

Most of these houses were once owned by Jewish people, several of whom were business owners who had gone north to communities such as Skokie, by the Dutch folks, a fair share of them blue-collar workers who had moved west to Cicero. By the time the Lawndale chapel had opened in the building, the neighborhood around it had begun to struggle. Businesses that had once thrived in the area began to flounder for various reasons; they closed their doors and fled, often leaving no place for people to make a decent living. And instead of the homes housing one family, as was the case previously, by the early 1960s, they often had extended families living in them so people could pool their resources to pay the bills. A bulk of the houses were owned by absentee landlords who had made a practice of charging exorbitant rents and who would mercilessly and suddenly evict families. Gangs such as the Vice Lords started to form, and drug dealers showed up on street corners. Some homes were gutted by fire or abandoned and boarded up. Alleys grew clogged with garbage. The Lawndale area, as these changes occurred, had started to gain "the reputation as an African American ghetto riddled with crime," writes Mulder in *White Flight*.[3]

A 1968 article in the *Chicago Daily News* reported that this was the most crime-ridden area in city. "In an average month, there are from 5 to 10 homicides, 30 to 35 rapes, between 600 and 900 felonies, and a call for police help every one-and-half minutes." But the reputation of being a hard, urban ghetto was not an obstacle for Clarence Buist, a graduate of Reformed Bible College in Grand Rapids. Working for the Chicagoland Board of Missions, and in the employ of Warren Park CRC in Cicero,[4] he made inroads into the community, forging close friendships as he spread the gospel, and the ministry saw results. Volunteers from area churches were recruited and taught Sunday school, led Bible classes, and ran youth programs.

"Soon there were Professions of Faith and Baptisms," Huiner continued. "Since Lawndale had not yet organized as a CR church, the memberships were registered at Warren Park, and members from Lawndale were warmly accepted at area churches." Lawndale, a community of about forty-five thousand people at the time, was organized as one of the first primarily black CRC congregations in 1963, with Huiner as pastor. Calling him to the positon made sense, given that he was familiar with the community, having grown up in nearby Cicero as the son of a successful scrap dealer.

---

[3]    P. 45.

[4]    Organized in 1899 as Douglas Park in Chicago, in 1927 it moved to Cicero as Second CRC, in 1956 it became Warren Park, Cicero, and in 1973 was discontinued with membership merged into Cicero, West Suburban, and in 1978 became Faith, Elmhurst, Chicago. *Historical Directory*, 23, 36.

Peter and Tona Huiner with
their children, *l-r*: Gregory,
Anne, and Miriam
(*courtesy Tona Huiner*)

Before coming to Lawndale, he had attended Calvin Theological Seminary (graduating while serving at Lawndale) and then worked for a time as an intern at Manhattan CRC, the inner-city ministry in Harlem which was a training ground for many ministers who would go on to serve in urban churches elsewhere.

Lawndale's members were worshipping in the small chapel at the former institute when the new pastor arrived but soon expanded into the gymnasium. Summer programs, writes Huiner,

Backyard Bible Story Time
(*courtesy Duane VanderBrug*)

boomed, filled with young people from the area and led by denominational youth teams. Barbara Campbell Otten recalled the early days of the church; she has especially fond memories of Huiner and his wife, Tona. "I loved Lawndale," she says. "I lived four houses down from the parsonage. I would walk past, and Pastor Peter and Tona would speak to me, take time with me, and give me books to read." She was the regular babysitter for the Huiner children. At the invitation of the Huiners, Campbell Otten attended a Backyard Bible Story Time. After that, she asked her parents if she could go to Lawndale CRC for services on Sundays, and they agreed. "Lawndale helped me to get to know the Lord better," she said. "The people there were very kind. It was at Lawndale that I started to be able to have hope for the future."

# CHAPTER 6

# Parents Seek Schooling for Their Children

From the start, Lawndale was a neighborhood church, drawing black families who had hope for a better future for themselves and their children. Tough as the area was, they were not about to give up and allow criminals and urban blight to overwhelm them. Many had a background in Baptist or independent churches and were attracted to the CRC's faithful, biblical teaching and values. When they learned of it, they were also attracted by the Reformed perspective that teaches involvement of one's faith in all of life. In addition, they lived in an area of Chicago in which a sense of the significance of fighting for civil rights—in schools, housing, and other areas—hung in the air. Martin Luther King Jr. was drawn to this neighborhood. In 1966 he set up his northern headquarters and co-chaired the Chicago Freedom Movement in Lawndale, attracted by both its problems

Rev. Robert Price
(*Archives, Calvin College*)

and its potential, says a *Chicago Tribune* article published in 2016 to mark the fiftieth anniversary of King's move to Lawndale.

But King was not the only civil rights activist at work in this gritty part of Chicago. Many pastors and Christian organizations, as well as the Black Panthers, the Nation of Islam, and other groups were here stirring the pot for change, adding to the highly charged atmosphere for seeking civil rights, said Rev. Robert Price, the CRC's director of Black and Urban Ministries. "King had a strong following, especially in his fight for fair housing," said Price, who grew up in the Chicago area. "But there were plenty of other groups organizing and doing things in Lawndale at the time."

It was during this period of heady optimism and hopes for civil rights that Peter Huiner began to speak and preach to parents about the value of their children receiving a Christian education at the nearby Timothy Christian Elementary School. This struck a chord; they were seeking a way out for their kids, and a good education promised it. They could see how others in

Pastor Duane VanderBrug in Lawndale CRC study, 1967
(*courtesy John Steigenga*)

the CRC were successful and hoped that a Christian education for their children could offer them the same success.

"I know from my pastoral relations with the congregation that the dominant and prevailing conviction and passion of the black Lawndale parents was to secure Christian education for their growing kids," said Duane VanderBrug, who came to Lawndale on June 1, 1966. At the time he arrived, the parents had applied to have their children attend Timothy but had not yet been turned down. "When the parents became members of the Lawndale CRC, they entered a whole new world of grace-possibilities for them and their families." Despite their desire to send their children to Timothy, the parents hesitated for a time. Reservations over what this might mean and the ramifications of what it might entail held them back. But Huiner continued to talk about it, emphasizing that Christian education was an important aspect of the CRC faith.

Huiner, an alumnus of Timothy Christian School, whose father, Bernard Huiner, at one time was the president of the board of Timothy, spoke often from the pulpit and in other settings about the bedrock value of Christian education; it was woven deeply into CRC belief and practice he told parents. It was a key avenue in which the teachings that took place on Sunday could be extended throughout the week in classrooms, where subjects were taught with Christ in mind. Other churches, such as the Reformed Church in America, believed otherwise. They taught that attending public schools was best; it helped to build solid citizens. But the CRC, writes Mark Mulder, took the other approach: God should be part of life at all times. In addition, Christian schools were a way to protect and promote the culture of the CRC.

Huiner says parents likely balked at first at sending their children for a very practical reason. "These schools are costly, and many of the people had limited financial means," he writes. But eventually the parents decided that making the sacrifice—and for many it would be substantial—would be worth it and got behind the idea. They also turned in this direction because of another practical reason: the neighborhood public schools were failing; they were simply warehouses for students instead of places of education. Classrooms were crowded; teachers lacked materials, and fighting was frequent.

Along with his familiarity with the Lawndale/Cicero area, Huiner had another personal connection drawing him to the issue of racial equity: he and his wife had adopted a minority child. Huiner lived what he believed, and this was clear to the members of Lawndale. "The people loved Peter, and they respected who he was and what he had to say, especially about the issue of Christian discipleship," said VanderBrug. "They knew the presence of their black kids in Timothy would integrate the school, but that was not their primary motive in seeking admission. For them (as the church council kept framing the struggle), it was their *Christian discipleship* that mattered. The right of their children to receive a good Christian education in the school closest to them is what motivated them."

Huiner and the parents were realistic. They knew that enrolling in nearby Timothy Christian School would likely pose challenges. But they were confident there was nothing they could not overcome. The theology of the church made it clear: God sought to show his love and acceptance to his covenant people in all things, including education. And so they made their first formal request in April 1965, when Huiner called Alfred Kieft, Timothy school board president, for a meeting regarding twenty-one students who wanted to be enrolled in the fall.

But in June, the parents were given a painful—and surprising—setback. After their meeting, the executive committee of the Timothy board told the parents that they could not admit their children. Board members were fearful that, if they allowed black children into the school, Cicero, known for its racist attitudes, would erupt in violence. This could go so far as harming the Lawndale students themselves. They also said that enrolling the students could cause parents who had children at Timothy to withdraw support.

Following this, the Lawndale council informed its regional church body, Classis Chicago North, that it was doing all it could to encourage a Christian education for their children. In the process, the council told classis, parents had applied at Timothy, and the school refused entry to their children. Although it did little to publicize its stance, preferring to stay out of the limelight, the board did explain its unwillingness to allow the children to enroll and integrate the school in an edition of the *Timothy Reflector*, the school's newsletter: "As trustees we are to see that our Covenant children receive the richest academic learning that is available along God-centered lines. To fit the Lawndale children into our school and to be faithful to the above commitments is beyond our capabilities at this time."

In another newsletter, they wrote: "We feel that this position in no way evidences a lack of faith on the part of the Board. An important part of faith is knowledge. This is both knowledge of the head as well as of the heart and involves sanctified common sense as well as the emotions. One must be extremely careful in judging matters of this nature on the basis of faith, lest we fall into the serious error of judging motives. We must above all avoid extremes in this highly volatile atmosphere."

An article in *Chimes*, the Calvin College newspaper, reported it with a different twist: "The school board justified its refusal of the Lawndale parents' request on the grounds that the community in which the school was located could be hostile to the presence of these children in their city. The cause of the refusal . . . the children are black."

Although the doors were closed at the elementary school, things were different at the Timothy Christian High School in Elmhurst, where, early in 1966, Lawndale parents petitioned the school board to admit a few students. After some heated discussions, they were accepted and enrolled in the suburban school. Even so, the lines had been drawn in Cicero, where the Christian school supported by the CRC was being forced to face up to the matter of race. And as it did, at least in the opinion of Rev. James La Grand, Timothy was not alone.

# CHAPTER 7

# Racism Infects the Christian School Movement

James La Grand[1] served as a teacher and missionary in Nigeria for two years in the early 1960s before returning with his family to the United States to attend Calvin Seminary. After graduating with his MDiv degree, he took a call in 1969 to serve as the first ordained pastor of what had been Garfield Chapel and was now becoming a newly organized CRC congregation. By then, the struggle at nearby Timothy was nearly four years old. "My dad didn't really know much about the situation at Timothy when he got there, but, as soon as he learned what was happening, he got involved," said David La Grand, James' son.

James La Grand led the opposition to the Timothy school board. Preaching from the pulpit and speaking out at classis and

---

[1]   Calvin Theological Seminary 1975; ordained 1969; Garfield, Chicago; All Nations, Halifax, NS, 1977-87; teacher, Chicago Metropolitan Center, Chicago, 1991-92; faculty, Lutheran School of Theology, Chicago, 1993; Beacon Light Community, Gary, IN, 1993-; retired 2006.

Rev. James La Grand
(*courtesy Virginia La Grand*)

in writing, he blasted the board for not allowing children from Lawndale and Garfield to attend the school. James believed it was his duty as a Christian minister to join others in battling the board. He was convinced that fighting racism at the school must be done relentlessly, according to his son, David, a Grand Rapids attorney, who was elected to serve in the Michigan Legislature in 2016.

James La Grand, in fact, "was a courageous and outspoken defender of racial justice and diversity in the church and society," wrote Janet Greidanus in the *Banner* after La Grand died on July 4, 2015. "La Grand was fearless and passionate as he worked for the church's witness to the gospel." La Grand never flagged in his belief that all of God's children deserve a Christian education, having come from a family in which his grandfather helped to found and raise money for Grand Rapids Christian High School, which James La Grand and other family members, including his son, attended. Soon after he arrived at Garfield, James wrote an article for the Reformed periodical *Christian Home and School*, which passionately described the racism afflicting Christian schools.

Sunday at Garfield CRC, with John La Grand and Tony Butler, *left to right*: Rev. James La Grand, Maria Butler, AnnaBelle Patterson, Robert Butler, 1974 (*courtesy Virginia La Grand*)

"My father argued all along that full racial reconciliation in all areas of life, including in education, is crucial if you are to define yourself as a Christian," said David La Grand, who is also a commissioned pastor in the CRC. "Absolutely, Christian education was a big deal for him. He was deeply dedicated to it."

Both his father and members of the Garfield chapel remained unbending allies of Lawndale in the fight to integrate Timothy. In fact, Garfield members would eventually join forces with Lawndale to form the Chicago West Side Christian School. "I was one of the first students at West Side," said David La Grand. "I attended there when it only had a kindergarten."

James La Grand left Garfield in 1974 and went on to earn a doctorate in New Testament at the University of Basel in Switzerland. He eventually turned his doctoral dissertation into the award-winning *Earliest Christian Mission to "All Nations" in Light of Matthew's Gospel*, a book that had the topic of the reconciliation of all people at its heart. He also served other CRC churches, including All Nations CRC in Halifax, Nova Scotia, and Beacon Light Community in Gary, Indiana. In the process, he was on different CRC boards and committees and became a resounding voice in the CRC in calling for an end to apartheid in South Africa. He also was a fierce advocate for women to be given the right to serve as ordained ministers in the CRC.[2]

But he also left his mark during his ministry in the West Chicago area. Before he moved on, he brought his faith to bear many times, and in various settings, in the struggle with the school in Cicero. On one occasion, La Grand stormed out of a classis meeting in protest when delegates to classis (he was not a delegate) failed to call the actions of the Timothy board sinful. Several times he spoke to the Timothy board and offered, along with Rev. Richard Grevengoed,[3] then pastor at Lawndale, to walk Lawndale/Garfield students to Timothy Christian School and stand there to protect them as they went in. But the board never took them up on the offer. In addition, La Grand was instrumental in helping to file the federal lawsuit in 1972 that charged Timothy with civil rights violations.

"Jim was a brilliant man who had very strong opinions," said Rev. Paul Kortenhoven,[4] a longtime friend and a former CRC missionary to Nigeria and Sierra Leone. "He wasn't always the gentlest of men and could be very confrontational. But he had a deep passion for the poor and for justice."

In 1969 La Grand wrote the article that for many people helped to encapsulate and highlight the social and theological issues underlying the fight between Lawndale and Garfield parents and the Timothy school board. Published in *Christian Home and School*, "The Christian School Movement Under Judgment" argues

---

[2]    *Historical Directory*, 265.

[3]    Immanuel, Roseville, MI, 1967; Lawndale, Chicago, 1970; Helping Hand Mission, Chicago, IL, 1981; New Leaf Resources, Lansing, IL, 1983; First Reformed Church, South Holland, IL, 2013; retired, 2006; MC, Elmhurst, IL.

[4]    Calvin Theological Seminary, BD, 1972; ordained 1972; missionary to Nigeria, 1972-75; Milbrook Christian School, Grand Rapids, MI, 1975-77; Community, St. Cloud, MN, 1977-80; missionary, Sierra Leone, 1980-2002, CRWM, Grand Rapids, 2002-8; retired.

Dr. Donald Opperwal
(*Archives, Calvin College*)

that the fight for equality in Christian education was not limited to the battle over the school in Cicero. La Grand was addressing the entire movement, which, according to Donald Oppewal, Calvin College education professor, traced its roots back to the seventeenth century in the Netherlands and took on a life of its own in the CRC in 1892 when Synod adopted a resolution favoring the organization of a society for the promotion of Christian Reformed education.

Drawing support from those seeking to eradicate racism in Christian schools at that time, La Grand's article gave a searing overview of the forces then impacting the CRC-supported system of schools. In it, he took the schools to task for their racism. What he saw happening in Christian education was unbiblical and sinful, he contended. For some reason, he did not specifically cite Timothy in his article. Maybe he did not want his argument to get lost by focusing on the school. Whatever the case, the struggle in Cicero was at the core of what he wrote. It was obvious that what was happening in his own backyard illustrated something much larger that was taking place in Christian education in the sixties.

This was an era, he points out, in which many Christian schools were struggling, really for the first time in their history, with the issue of race. Some schools, and in these limited cases often reluctantly, had opened their doors to minorities living in their communities. But many Christian schools had become part of the problem, instead of the solution. As parents sought to enroll minority children in these schools, La Grand contended, the schools and their school boards faced pressure causing them to react in ways "which threaten to remake the Christian school movement in the racist's image." These pressures, he wrote, had caused "two new patterns which had become so well established as to indicate a new direction in the (Christian school) movement."

The first pattern was the flight of schools from inner cities to outlying, less populated areas. He did not mention it, but this is what Timothy did when it moved its high school to Elmhurst. "The second pattern," La Grand went on, "is the outright refusal to admit black Covenant children to schools which bear the name 'Christian.' Both patterns encourage racism, and both are symptoms of sickness in the movement." La Grand also said Christian schools missed the mark when they referred to themselves as being "private." By seeking to call themselves private, and in some cases going so far as to petition for government funding as private schools, the Christian-school movement was in danger of forgetting its own roots. Those roots, he argued, are based in the gospel and the truth that God is the keeper of the schools, not school boards. They are not really private or public; they are God's. Funding should come from people of faith, not government tax dollars

People had "slipped into the mistaken assumption that Christian schools are the property of those who paid for their construction" and that they could sell them whenever and to whomever they wished. "But the Scriptures speak plainly on this subject," says La Grand. "To use the name 'Christian' for private advantage is sin demanding repentance, 'For the Lord will not hold him guiltless who takes His name in vain'" (Deuteronomy 5:11). School boards that did not follow these truths, he argues, ran the risk of forsaking their purpose, which was to educate all of God's children. At its heart, the article charged that the Christian-school movement was veering into—if not already enmeshed in—dangerous territory.

# CHAPTER 8

# "Up the Up Staircase"

The article by James La Grand ruffled some feathers among Christian school leaders. They were not used to being put on the hot seat, with their Christian ethics called into question. Like much of the CRC, they had been insulated, often by their own design, from whatever problems were plaguing society at the time. They liked it that way; in fact, Christian schools and the parents who paid the tuition saw them as enclaves of stability, institutions dedicated to holding up values of CRC singularity.

But others appreciated the assessment provided by La Grand. His article helped to put the issues in focus, particularly about who really owned these schools. "They are God's schools, for God's children," said VanderBrug, who had served Manhattan CRC in Harlem in the early 1960s before being called to Lawndale. "And this is what we sincerely believed throughout the entire process.

Rev. Duane VanderBrug, 1967
(*courtesy John Steigenga*)

By placing too much attention on what the school board did or didn't do missed the point of what we wanted to accomplish."

Published in 1969, La Grand's article was in many ways a rallying cry that helped reflect what the Lawndale CRC council had been saying all along as it sought to have children admitted to Timothy. "From the beginning," said VanderBrug, "the Lawndale Council and Christian Education Committee kept framing the issue in terms of Christian discipleship—the call to follow Christ in living out the demands of the gospel in all of society."

The Lawndale council believed this was the calling it must pursue. But the council had another reason for pushing this approach. Board members believed, in the context of discipleship, Timothy Christian school board members could answer the call of Christ and find reasons to take a courageous, biblical stand and admit the children. The church council hoped, said VanderBrug, the school board would be able to see it had a deeper duty that went well beyond bricks and mortar and even the potentially explosive circumstances of Cicero. School board members hopefully would see they had a duty to set aside their race-based attitudes for the greater good of Christ's commands and for the enduring welfare of the children. By doing this, they could justify opening their doors to the Lawndale children and basically take the high ground. But this argument never swayed the Timothy board.

At the request of the Lawndale council, VanderBrug wrote two articles, titled "Up the Up Staircase," for the *Banner* on the school issue and Christian discipleship. He laid out his own arguments for why a Christian school should act in accordance with the beliefs it professed. In the May 24, 1968, edition of the CRC's periodical, VanderBrug wrote that Christ called his people to reach out to one another in love; this meant making room in schools such as Timothy for children of all races to get a Christian education. But there was something else as well. It also meant that Lawndale parents had the responsibility to pursue what God would have them do, which was to seek a Christian education for their children, regardless of how hard it was to be continually turned down. They had their own calling to heed. In the end, wrote VanderBrug, the issue was not race but accepting the will and sovereignty of God; it was about following God's desire for building unity and working for reconciliation in all of society. It was about blacks and whites sitting in the classroom and learning about God's world together. It was about something that transcended Timothy.

"The issue was really about Christian discipleship, whether we all had the courage and faith to do the right thing in the face of opposition," VanderBrug wrote, going on in his article to specifically cite Timothy and the town in which it stood as thwarting the call to discipleship. "And the point of the debate was whether God chose or we chose the point at which we would risk ourselves in obedience to the Lord in this unfriendly town." They chose, he went on to write, to follow God's leading, which was to keep working to have the children accepted into the school, regardless of the perceived danger. As for the Timothy school board, "Its decision denying admission remains in spite of it being challenged because its ground is not valid for a Christian community." Despite their ongoing feelings of rejection, said VanderBrug in an interview, Lawndale parents could take solace in knowing they were doing the right thing. They were following God's leading to be his disciples and, difficult and traumatic as it might be, they were not about to give up. They kept trying. But the only problem in repeatedly working to get their children into Timothy was dealing with this obstacle known as Cicero.

# CHAPTER 9

# What Was It about Cicero?

Today Cicero is a highly urbanized area with nearly eighty-five thousand people, more than 85 percent of whom are Hispanic, per estimated US census data for 2014. The city shows the signs of transition and struggle familiar in many inner cities. Bustling restaurants, meat markets and groceries, and other enterprises run for decades by prosperous local families have been replaced by small strip malls featuring cash advance franchises, low-cost haircut salons, fast-food restaurants, and liquor stores that double up selling lottery tickets. Self-storage places and small industrial centers are also here. Some larger businesses have closed; others such as a shoe manufacturer and a railway company remain.

In the mid-1860s, when it was incorporated, the city was populated by only a smattering of upwardly mobile white families moving there from nearby Chicago. Mirroring the demographic of white flight that has remained steady over the decades, they

Dr. Robert P. Swierenga
at the podium at Calvin College
(*Archives, Calvin College*)

sought the comfort of an outlying area which, in this case, had been the site of small truck farms and was now being filled by "brick bungalows with tree-lined sidewalks and backyard gardens," writes historian Robert P. Swierenga in his article "Masselink[1] Challenges the Cicero Mob," published in *Origins*.[2]

Businesses sprang up, notably factories which manufactured telephone equipment and switching materials for the Bell system and a company that built farm equipment. Sears Roebuck, the huge, mail-order enterprise, sprouted up nearby. As Cicero grew, hundreds of workers from across the area found jobs; many sought to move into the community. To accommodate and respond to the needs of this influx of people, taverns, grocery stores, churches, schools, and other organizations and businesses opened.

Cicero had no history or reputation in its early years of opposing integration. But as the population grew, things began to change. By the early decades of the twentieth century, thousands of working-class Czechoslovakian, Lithuanian, Polish, and Italian descendants had joined a handful of Dutch Reformed families to

---

[1]    Edward Johann Masselink, Princeton Theological Seminary, BA; University of Chicago, MA; Southern Baptist Theological Seminary, ThD, 1927; ordained, 1927; Trinity Reformed, RCA, Grand Rapids, MI, 1927-29; CRC: Burton Heights, Grand Rapids, 1929-40; LaGrave Ave., Grand Rapids; 1940-44; First Cicero, IL, 1944-50; Twelfth St., Grand Rapids, 1950-55; Central Ave., Holland, MI, 1955-62; Thirty-Sixth St., Wyoming, MI, 1962-66; retired, 1966; *Historical Directory*, 276.

[2]    *Origins* 24, no. 1 (2006), 36ff.

settle in Cicero, writes Swierenga.[3] Many were seeking work, but they were also fleeing their former neighborhoods, having been chased out by "unscrupulous realtors" who were moving black families into the previously all-white, Chicago neighborhoods in order to create fear and spark white flight and a rapid decline in home prices.

This practice, known as blockbusting, has been used repeatedly over the years in Chicago and elsewhere as a way for realtors to sell white families newer homes for higher prices and bigger profits in supposedly safer neighborhoods. While this practice may have made better homes more accessible for blacks, it also caused problems for the white families who moved, especially in the case of Cicero. Many of these families held a grudge, says Swierenga, quoting a CRC pastor who said these working-class folks associated blacks with the loss of their previous homes in Chicago.

Now that they were in their new houses, Cicero residents feared that if blacks moved in, they would be forced out. And they were not going to be pushed out again. They vowed to stand their ground against what they saw as an overwhelming onslaught of urban change. But fear of becoming victims of blockbusting was only part of what helped shape the psyche and attitudes of people in Cicero. They also lived in a community that had a long history of criminal activity. The notorious gangster Al Capone had lived there. He had built his criminal empire in Chicago before moving to Cicero to escape the reach of the Chicago police. Following behind, came fellow crooks who moved into the well-to-do, Chicago-style, brick bungalows—homes with small, peaked roofs, detailed windows, and neatly manicured lawns. Once they settled in, they built various illegal enterprises in the process shaping the personality of the town and especially the politics.

---

[3] Ibid., 37.

Rev. Ed. Masselink
(*Archives, Calvin College*)

"For most of the twentieth century, there were direct links between town hall and the mob. [For] most of the twentieth century, town hall didn't hesitate to strong arm anybody. If city officials decided they didn't like you, you obeyed, you suffered, or you got out of town," said National Public Radio host Ira Glass in 2000 for his show *This American Life*, which ran a series profiling the town. Ira Glass also said, "For decades, Cicero was this place that did not want outsiders moving in. [It] fought violently against blacks and other minorities coming into town."

In his *Origins* article, Swierenga tells the story of Rev. Edward Masselink, a CRC minister and host of the popular radio program, *Reformation Hour*, to illustrate the corrupt nature of city hall. Masselink, pastor of First CRC in Cicero, according to Swierenga, was deeply troubled by how the mob controlled the city, causing graft, greed, and activities such as prostitution, gambling, and after-hours bars to run rampant. Disregarding his own safety, Masselink spoke out against Capone and other mobsters. Not surprisingly, this incurred the wrath of Capone's people. One mobster even said that if the minister did not keep his mouth shut, he would be "riding out of town on a slab."

There were other threats. But Masselink was not deterred. In early 1948, he led a group of ministers on a campaign to get their own man, John Stoffel, elected town president of Cicero. To their credit, Stoffel won. And once he was in office, Masselink and the other pastors sent a strongly worded statement to the Cicero town board. They wanted big changes, starting at city hall. Their statement came in the form of a resolution, listing changes, such as enforcing a 2:00 a.m. closing time in local saloons, which were needed to "clean up" Cicero. Once the resolution was read at the board meeting, says Swierenga, Masselink stood up to "declare the resolution was not simply empty words but a program of action." He and the other clergy "promised to make the crusade a matter of public and personal prayer, and they called on public-minded civic organizations and individuals to come and stand with them."

They fought hard to get the resolution seeking changes put on the ballot, but it failed to happen. The criminal elements which held the power blocked the measure, and the people of Cicero never had a chance to vote to transform their city. In the wake of this, Stoffel resigned, and the mob returned their man to office. After that, the resolve of the ministerial association lost steam. Masselink's congregation at First CRC generally stood by him through the struggle. But as things died down, says Swierenga, it became clear just how divided church members were by his civic activism. He left in the early 1950s to take a call at a church in Grand Rapids.

In 1951, about the time Masselink was leaving,[4] an incident occurred that highlighted the racial tensions which had been brewing in Cicero, along with so many other things. The Cicero Race Riot broke out when a mob of four thousand whites attacked an apartment building which was home to the

[4]　Masselink left Cicero in 1950; *Historical Directory*, 276.

Clarks, a black family who had moved into a white neighborhood. "On July 11, 1951, at dusk, a crowd of 4,000 whites attacked the apartment building that housed Clark's family and possessions,"[5] About sixty police officers assigned to the scene stood by and watched as rioters broke into the building and ransacked the place, destroying hallways, ripping up plaster, tearing out plumbing, smashing doors and windows, and setting fires. In the end, the governor had to call in the National Guard.

[5]    The *African American Registry*.

# CHAPTER 10

# CRC Life in Cicero

Despite racial tensions and other challenges, the CRC ministry was rich and vital in Cicero over the decades. Masselink and other pastors were examples of Christian men who fought on behalf of the people, living out the commands of Christ to advocate in all areas of life for the oppressed and needy. And the CRC congregations in Cicero and nearby worked in many ways to reach out to their neighbors. Evidence of this can be seen in the mission work among the Jewish population accomplished at the former Nathaniel Institute and the outreach in the founding of Lawndale CRC. The churches worked in other ways as well, starting chapels such as the Garfield Chapel[1] and reaching out with clothing and food to the poor in their neighborhoods. They also established many ministries to young people and worked with the homeless in nearby Chicago. They prayed for

[1]    Chicago, 1963-88.

their neighborhoods, and many CRC members operated local businesses, large and small, which employed hundreds of people throughout the area.

Yet, the reality was, the CRC community in Cicero remained insular, significantly set apart from the wider world. Church members in Cicero and across the Chicago area, writes Swierenga, "were 'tribal' in their fierce, in-group loyalties, behavior of exclusiveness, and the transplanting of Old Country institutions and the Dutch language and culture." This tribal quality did, however, offer stability to the community.

Peter Huiner recalls Cicero being a close-knit, deeply religious area. Families attended church twice on Sunday and gathered at each other's homes regularly for fellowship. Life revolved around their faith. Deep friendships were formed and maintained. People vacationed together, attended weekly Bible studies, and married within their denomination. They did mission work together. Young people joined the Young Calvinist League, the CRC alternative to the secular Boy Scouts and Girl Scouts. Most went to Christian schools, which were governed by CRC "societies." Operated in this manner, the schools remained autonomous from the denomination, unlike the private Catholic schools which were owned and operated by the church. "Anchoring the whole lives of the second and third generation immigrants were the trinity of 'Kingdom causes': the church, the Christian school, and missionary work," Huiner writes in his foreword "Out of Cicero."

Church life in Cicero affected Huiner and his ministry in powerful ways. His childhood memories of church and school are full of the friends he met there, what they did together, and how their days were shaped by a faith that seemed sure and unshakable. They played on sports teams, attended social functions at their churches, and experienced the comfort of learning about a faith that defined so much of what they did and

First Cicero Christian Reformed Church (artist's rendering)
(*Archives, Calvin College*)

how they viewed life. They lived in a city with well-ordered streets which was comfortable and safe. Their faith was a haven from which they rarely ventured. The issue of race, although hovering, did not intrude as Huiner grew up.

There was also, however, a painful downside to this tribalism. It was traumatic, says Huiner, when former friends became enemies after he returned to Cicero from Manhattan CRC and became pastor of Lawndale and encouraged parents to enroll their children in Timothy. Huiner was shocked by the intense reaction to the church's attempt to integrate the school. He received hateful, threatening phone calls and letters from leaders in the CRC community, including members of the school board. He experienced first-hand the ambiguity of Cicero and the CRC community which had bred passionate pastors such as Masselink and offered stability to church members but also punished people who threatened the status quo. But Huiner was not the only one who suffered. His father, Bernard, a scrap dealer in Cicero, also became a target of the hatred. People turned on the elder Huiner, even though he had served for many years on the Timothy school board. Both of his parents became targets of scorn, despite the fact they "gave the school a lot of money," Huiner says. "My parents went to the same church as Timothy board members. They were socially ostracized after this. After my dad died in '68, my mom had to move away from Cicero."

People on each side of the divide—many of them close friends for years—had a difficult time throughout the struggle. Their lives were wrenched apart; relationships were severed for good. Hardly anyone emerged unscathed. CRC members pushed on in their lives, sharing the same faith, but they found themselves at odds with one another. They experienced cracks in their once predictable culture, defined in so many ways by their ethnic heritage. The church community in which they had taken refuge and from which they received so much comfort had become a breeding ground for strife.

Hurt by the very people with whom he once attended catechism, school, and church, Peter Huiner himself had to leave the area, not long after coming to Lawndale CRC and pushing for integration of Timothy. In fact, he eventually left the CRC altogether in 1970 to study for ordination as an Episcopal priest.

# CHAPTER 11

# It May Be Lawful, but . . .

As we have described it, the Timothy Christian School controversy had its roots in a checkered history of families who had memories of blockbusting, criminals who ran the city for their own purposes, a race riot, and churches facing the realities of a changing culture. Without these mitigating factors, without the stark reality that Cicero was Cicero, the confrontation between parents and the school board may have taken a different track. If nothing else, perhaps it would not have been so acrimonious.

There are those who say the board's unwillingness to open the doors to Lawndale children was outright racism, an effort to deny civil rights to blacks, which reflected the community's overriding and long-held attitudes. But it can also be argued, that things were much more complicated than that. Members of the school board were men of faith and conviction; they were not villains who had no good reason for taking the stance they did.

For instance, one woman, who taught seventh-grade at

Trucks looted in front of the church after the snowstorm of 1967
(*courtesy Duane VanderBrug*)

Timothy in 1966, said she has compassion for the school officials who had to deal with the tension and troubles. The school was located in a neighborhood in which a mobster lived. But the neighborhood itself, in which she lived with some other teachers, was peaceful.

> The population of that neighborhood was made up of various ethnic groups living side by side. Everyone knew there was a mobster living in the area, but he was a good citizen in the neighborhood. Some of my students went to his house when they were doing a fund raising for the school. They were not afraid of him, and he did give a contribution. Even so, there was the underlying racial tension and other issues.[1]

The teacher also recalls the day near the end of the 1965-66 school year on which parents from Lawndale were scheduled

---

[1]    Interview with Timothy teacher, January 6, 2017, who even now declines to be named.

to make a visit to the school that night. Someone had called in a bomb threat, which included both the school and First CRC across the street.

> The threat was called in on a nice warm day. The principal called the staff together to explain that a bomb threat had been called in. No one knew where it came from. We refused to cancel and all agreed that we were going to go ahead with the conferences. We surely were blessed that nothing happened.

The bomb threat was a disturbing example of the nature of the community and of the stark dilemma with which school officials had to contend. "You can't put your own opinions on them [school officials] from the outside without really understanding what they were up against," said the teacher.

Clearly, deeper motivations, including threats of violence, combined with social trends, were at work in Cicero. In many ways, school officials were caught between a troubled past, which included the race riot in 1951, and current threats of violence, such as the bomb threat. There were other instances as well of threats which probably worked to shape the attitudes of some residents of Cicero.

For instance, there was the "Garbage War" during the 1960s, in which the Italian mob tried to muscle in on the "multi-million-dollar, refuse business," from which many Dutch people made their living.[2]

"In 1960 syndicate leader William Daddano, alias 'Willie Potatoes,' formed a company, American Scavenger Service, in order to take over the private refuse business," said Swierenga. Daddano sent his men to long-time customers of the Dutch garbage

---

[2]  Robert P. Swierenga, "Garbios: Chicago's Dutch Scavengers," lecture presented at Calvin College Alumni Lectures, at Bradenton and Naples, Florida, Feb. 21 and 23, 2005.

collectors in Cicero and told them that the new company would take over their garbage pickups. "'All they [the mafia] do,' a Dutchman complained, 'is drop the name of a hood friend and they get the business—customers I had for years.'" When people stopped by to ask why customers canceled, "'All they tell us is,' said the Dutchman, 'is please go away, we don't want to have anything to do with you.'" Swierenga said the implied threat worked for a time. "With such strong-arm tactics, Daddano and his operatives in the first three months took from the Dutch more than one hundred of their best accounts—nightclubs, restaurants, and large stores."

This was an era in which Dutch folks—not just the garbage collectors—had reason to fear, especially in the matter of race relations. There were critics who said residents of Cicero, and particularly those who ran Timothy Christian School, were narrow minded and reactionary. But the truth is, many Timothy supporters had thought seriously about what they did, and they did not take their position lightly. Their struggle was multifaceted, taking into consideration the teachings of their Christian faith and the reality of the city in which they lived. We see that struggle outlined in a position paper, published as a small booklet in 1969, and distributed on Reformation Day to churches across Classis Chicago North.

Referring to a quote from 1 Cor. 10:23, the booklet was called *All Things Are Lawful; But Not All Things Are Expedient.* In it the board laid out its reasoning; reiterating racism was not at the core of why they continued to bar Lawndale children from the school. Rather, the board emphasized, it was Cicero with its long history of racial hostility that fueled its thinking. "The well-publicized racial events of recent years have only served to fan the flames of fear and prejudice, and Cicero today is more determined than ever to preserve its racially segregated status." Not even the Roman Catholic Archdiocese of Chicago, which sought racial equality in

# *"All Things Are Lawful,*
# *But Not All Things Are Expedient"*

### A POSITION PAPER

### TIMOTHY CHRISTIAN SCHOOL BOARD

### CICERO, ILLINOIS, OCTOBER, 1969

Four years ago, in April, 1965, the Timothy Christian School Board received a request from the parents of several black children, members of the Lawndale Christian Reformed Church in Chicago, for admission of these children into the Timothy Christian Schools. Their request was thoroughly reviewed by the Board, and it was decided that in view of the extreme racial tension which existed in the Town of Cicero, site of two of the Board's three schools, the parents request should not be granted at that time. One year later, the Board approved the enrollment of several Lawndale children in the high school, located in Elmhurst, Illinois, but decided again that conditions in Cicero would not permit the safe enrollment of Lawndale children in the Cicero schools. So began the controversy which still confronts us today.

The Reformed community, although uncomfortable about the inability to grant to Lawndale parents what seemingly was so basic a right, has firmly supported the Board's position from the outset, and even more firmly supports it today, particularly since other means have been found to provide Christian education for Lawndale chil-

Position paper of the Timothy school board, 1969
(*Archives, Calvin College*)

Snowstorm of 1967 covering the looting and burning of stores
just down the blook from Lawndale Church
(*courtesy Duane VanderBrug*)

all its schools, wanted to locate a school in Cicero. Clearly, the forces against this kind of change were strongly allied against any real type of integration, as outlined in the booklet.

The booklet also clearly blames Huiner and VanderBrug for pushing an agenda that was not going to fly in a Cicero school. These pastors, the text claims, broke from a more traditional form of teaching and preaching the gospel and began "an aggressive program of social action. Church members were told of their repression by the white community and of the racial hatred that existed in the community, even among Christians. They were urged to stand up and fight for their rights, one of which was to enter the Christian Schools in Cicero." In other words, they were preaching a social gospel.

Along with providing a chronology of board action on the matter, the booklet underlines the dilemma it faced. Lawndale children had the right to an education in the Cicero school, but enrolling them was not practical; it would only lead to violence, which might mean the destruction of the school and all the work people had put into it for so many years. At the very least, it could cause parents to remove their students for fear of what might happen. "The practical result, then, of enrolling Lawndale children in Cicero, would be at best, a closing of the school due to withdrawal of students, and at worst, destruction of the school and/or its inhabitants. The reasons [to enroll Lawndale students under these circumstances] must be compelling indeed, in order to induce any School Board or its constituency to adopt policies so clearly suicidal."

The booklet also criticizes outside groups, such as Classis Chicago North and the CRC's Synod, for trying to force their views on a private, school board matter and trying to unfairly exploit and turn this into a national issue. Until publishing the position paper, the board said, it had kept a low profile. "All of the board's efforts . . . have been made quietly and within the confines of the local community. In spite of many rash statements made to us and about us, we have turned the other cheek without making any public response." But the board decided it had to put its side of the story before the public.

The board says near the end of the position paper that it did not blame Lawndale parents for seeking to enroll their children. "They bear very little, if any, responsibility for the present controversy." These parents were misinformed about why their children were barred from the school, and it was not a kingdom matter, but a matter of expediency, on which the board made its decisions. At the same time, however, Lawndale parents would need to sort this through, says the position paper, and "must someday make their own accounting" for how they reacted to the situation.

James Schaap published a blog in mid-2014 reflecting on the controversy. He was a college student at the time of the fight over integration at Timothy and followed it closely. Although he does not mention the position paper, Schaap offers insight into the struggle in his blog. He writes of participating in a breakfast meeting with some of the former Timothy school board members, a meeting at which he says he suspected, after so many years, they would have had a chance to look back and express remorse for refusing to admit black students. By then, Schaap thought, they would have seen the error of their ways. But he had it wrong. "Each one claimed that if he had to determine an answer to the request of those black parents again back then, if he had to relive all that hate, his answer would be the same. Each of them was absolutely sure that horror would result, not from African Americans, but from their own white neighbors. That is how much hate they witnessed and feared."

It was Cicero, with its long history of racial and social conflict, just as the board argued in the 1969 position paper, that had led to fear and to their decisions. But underlying their actions was a truth troubling to Schaap. These men had failed to treat the children fairly as fellow members of the CRC. They had allowed a prevailing sense of prejudice in the community to override their Christian convictions and to reject children of the covenant. In his blog, Schaap writes, "Back then, were they right? I think not. But there's far more hesitation in my voice when I say that, fifty years later."

Thinking of those men with whom he met and of how his own thoughts had changed since the upheaval of the 1960s, he writes, "I understand them far better than I did when I was twenty because I've heard their memories and their life stories both before and after the Timothy crisis. I listened to their testimony of faith. I saw tears. I felt in all of those stories the very real humanity of those men, which is to say, by way of my faith, I felt the image of God right there in them as they sat and talked around that breakfast table."

Ralph Lubben
(*courtesy John Steigenga*)

Rev. R. Kooistra, a writer for *Calvinist-Contact Christian Weekly*, had a chance to speak with ministers who had served in Chicago during this period. They essentially told him that the Timothy Christian school board was dealing with a complex matter that could not be easily summed up as being bad or good. They told Kooistra that Cicero had been corrupt for many years and remained corrupt and was run by "a so-called Syndicate." These ministers said this group of crooks ran things as it wanted, putting the school board in a tough place. "It seems that these unknown, uncrowned rulers control the established bodies of authority: City Council, Police Force and Fire Department," Kooistra wrote in the Christian weekly in 1969. If that was true, nothing short of transforming the entire power structure of Cicero could have made it safe for the Lawndale children to attend Timothy, he wrote. So even if the police were called in to provide protection, which the school board never asked to have happen, it is probably worth wondering if the police would have followed through or stepped aside just as they did during the riot in 1951.

As she looks back on that time, Gladys Lubben still feels sad over the tension that existed among members of the CRC over Timothy. She and her husband, Ralph, lived in the western suburb of Maywood, just beyond Berwyn. As two of the few Anglo members of Lawndale, the Lubbens were strong supporters of integrating the school. Because their children were white, they were able to attend Timothy in their early years. Later, Ralph and Gladys enrolled their children at Des Plaines. For she and her husband, a sign painter who is deceased, it was the division among friends that was so difficult and continues to grieve her, regardless of the reasoning for keeping the school closed to blacks. She knew people on the Timothy board as being deeply religious and committed to the CRC faith. She knew many believed strongly that what they were doing was right. "This situation involved people I had known all of my life, and they were good people. I'm not sure God wanted it to have been so messy, although we know God is in charge and out of all things comes good," she said.

# CHAPTER 12

# The Big Yellow School Bus

Still committed to their cause, Lawndale parents once again petitioned the Timothy school board to admit their children for the 1967 school year. But the board rejected them outright. This is the point, says VanderBrug, at which the Lawndale church began seriously to look for alternatives and ended up asking if the Des Plaines Christian School would admit their children.

To help smooth the way, Rev. John Draisma,[1] pastor of Des Plaines CRC, where the Des Plaines Christian School was located, visited many of the homes in the neighborhood of the church and school to explain to them why the school wanted to admit black students. No survey was taken of the neighbors as Timothy had done at one point, and no controversy emerged, likely in part due to Draisma's house-to-house canvassing. In short order, the Des

---

[1]  Calvin Theological Seminary, BD, 1959; ordained 1959; Parkersburg, IA, 1959-62; First Des Plaines, IL, 1962-68, Holland Heights, Holland, MI, 1968-75; d. 1975.

Rev. John Draisma
(*Archives, Calvin College*)

Plaines board made the decision, based on Christian principles, that these were God's children and should be invited to attend the school.

After the Des Plaines board informed him of its decision, VanderBrug sent a letter to church members in which he wrote: "Last Monday evening, the Lord opened an exciting possibility to us when the Des Plaines School Board informed us that they would receive our children to be in their Christian grade school." Everyone was excited. But, soon, reality set in. Having to travel to Des Plaines meant that the church would need to obtain a school bus and come up with the money to maintain it.

"First, it was a loaner, a very old bus," recalls VanderBrug. "When it broke down once every other week, the state police would call me. This was before cell phones, which made things more complicated." Then, a company unexpectedly sold the church a new Bluebird bus for $6,000; the church had only $1,000 in the bank, but they received help from other churches, several in Classis Chicago North and some from as far away as Washington, DC, and New York City. Even patients from Pine Rest Christian Hospital in Grand Rapids joined area churches and chipped in to help make the payments. And their children—at first twenty and then thirty-six grade-school children, thirty-one black and five Anglo—reaped the benefits of being able to ride the new Bluebird bus to go to the school where racial harmony was celebrated.

One of the bus drivers was Dorothy J. Ritchie, a long-time member of Lawndale CRC. She said that she deeply appreciates all the work VanderBrug did in fighting to get her children and other black children a Christian education. Although she agreed to drive the bus, she recalled, she had to learn how to operate a stick shift. "So, who but Duane taught me how to do a stick shift?" He was patient with her, and, she says, "When I graduated, he must have thought I did all right because he and Adele (his wife) allowed their youngest child, Maria, to ride along with me anytime I asked her if she wanted to go. So she was a very good sweet little mascot."

She particularly remembers an incident during the second school year on the day Martin Luther King was assassinated, and riots broke out across the country, including in Chicago and, most notably, on Roosevelt Road, just a block from Lawndale CRC. Not long after, word circulated that King had been killed, and the area erupted. Businesses—many owned by Jewish merchants—along Roosevelt were ransacked, and white people were dragged out of their cars and beaten. VanderBrug and John Steigenga, who served as a pastoral intern at the church, had to lay low as rioters broke into and burned buildings. Flames from some structures leapt as high as the tree tops; looters pushing shopping carts of food and other things from a nearby supermarket moved down Springfield Avenue in Lawndale. Not wanting to venture too close to Lawndale CRC during these scary days, VanderBrug and Steigenga held the Sunday service at nearby Wheaton CRC. But because things were so tense, says Ritchie, VanderBrug did go out and, leaving behind their smoke-filled neighborhood, intercepted her as she was driving toward Des Plaines the day after King died.

Maria, Adele, Sharon, and
Chip VanderBrug, 1967
(*courtesy Duane VanderBrug*)

After stopping the bus, VanderBrug informed her he had a plan
to protect the children in case they encountered any violence. But
they did not need the plan. "We were very fortunate not to have
run into any problems," says Ritchie. "We knew that the Lord had
us in his hands."

At the same time, she recalls, just in case they might be in
danger riding on a bus with white children, she had told Chip and
Sharon, Duane and Adele VanderBrug's children, to hide under
the seats, cover themselves with a blanket, and not show their
white faces. "Chip remembers that well," says Duane VanderBrug.

As mentioned, the transition into the Des Plaines school
went smoothly. The presence of the Lawndale children among
the sixty students at Des Plaines "has not created problems.
Instead, the children have been completely accepted," Raymond
Vander Molen, the school principal, told the *Chicago Sun Times*.
In the article, Vander Molen also said, "The kids are aware of
the color difference, but it really hasn't made any difference. We
did nothing to prepare our kids. They knew they were coming,
and that was it." Debra Brown, who now works for the Veteran's
Administration in Chicago, has fond memories of attending Des
Plains and especially of Vander Molen. He was a kind man and a
good teacher. She remembers how he taught three grades in one
room, rolling on his chair among the students throughout the
day. He took his time to explain things clearly to the new students.
"This school was very different, but we adapted," she said. She was
not enthusiastic about the long bus ride to and from the school

Des Plaines Christian School shared spaced with
the Des Plaines Christian Reformed Church
(*Des Plaines Christian Schools*)

and yet it gave all of them time to build friendships. "There was a lot of laughter and talking and joking. It built camaraderie. We were embraced pretty well by the school in Des Plaines. There was no racism problem."

Helen Peterson, a K-2 teacher at the school, served as a summer volunteer at Lawndale to get to know the children who would be attending Des Plaines in the fall. "She wanted to become familiar with the neighborhood the kids lived in," recalls VanderBrug. "It was a gracious way to help prepare herself for the Lawndale children in the Des Plaines school." In a letter, Peterson said that when the school year opened "There were many new faces, white and black, all representing God's children eager for a Christian education." As the school year unfolded, she was pleased to see "a wonderful blending of children and parents. It was fun to share Christian education (something I had taken for granted) with brothers and sisters who were enjoying it for the first time." To be sure, she notes, differences existed between students, teachers, and parents. "But we learned to enjoy and appreciate these differences." Having the Lawndale students among them added immeasurably to everyone's experiences throughout the year. She said she suspects the Lawndale students and their parents felt the same way. "Together we were one family learning, playing,

Lawndale 1967 summer staff, with Helen Peterson, *front left*
(*courtesy John Steigenga*)

praying, loving, and caring for each other during the year's events: potlucks, conferences, PTA, work projects, field trips, the Chicago racial riots, the death of a student, bazaars, school programs, and graduation."

# CHAPTER 13

# Looking beyond Des Plaines

The Lawndale parents were grateful for the opportunity to send their children to the school in Des Plaines, but it was hard. The long bus ride on busy freeways to and from the suburban school began taking a toll on the children. They left early and returned home late. In addition, it was becoming clear that the Des Plaines school, because of its small size, was going to have a hard time accommodating the more-than-thirty Lawndale students planning to attend in 1968-69. "I know my parents appreciated us being able to go to Des Plaines, but all along, they told me later, they wanted us to go to Timothy because it was so much closer," said Clarence "Doc" Taylor, a retired truck driver who now plays keyboard for the praise band at Lawndale CRC. His mother, Emma, was one of the bus drivers. "Even though they weren't having us [at Timothy], I know my parents kept trying. Getting a better education was real important," said Taylor.

Rev. John Steigenga
(*Archives, Calvin College*)

"Especially my dad wanted this to happen. He was not a half-way person. When he cared about something, he was all in, and so he kept fighting to get us in at Timothy."

His father, Clinton, a construction worker, was among those, then, who led the move to ask Timothy in 1968 to admit their children for the school year. They continued to believe that, along with the school being closer, this was a matter of Christian conscience and discipleship. It was their duty to keep asking the school for entry. But again, they were bluntly turned down, now for the third time. This time, though, it was different. Clarence Taylor and others were starting to lose their patience. And at the same time, they began to realize to their satisfaction they were not as alone as they had thought, because, increasingly, the situation was gaining a higher profile, and parents had a growing number of supporters.

For instance, Classis Chicago North had stepped up to stand with parents. The classis would later take a different stance. But in late 1967, it issued a statement that said: "It is the conviction of Classis that consistency with the faith we all profess requires that such children should be admitted. This is the direct implication of the Gospel on which the Christian School is based. . . . This may well entail sacrifice, but this stands at the heart of Christian discipleship."

Another supporter and advocate for parents was Rev. John Steigenga,[1] who grew up in rural Michigan and served as an intern at Lawndale between 1967-68. Whereas classis spoke publicly about the issue, Steigenga learned of it first hand, and it became part of his ministry. When he arrived at the church, he was a stranger to racism. But it did not take long for him to realize that the opportunity he had as a youth to attend Christian schools was being denied to the young people of Lawndale. "It was a rude awakening to the realities of racism to realize that the people I was coming to know and love in the Lawndale church could not do what my parents had done, namely enroll their children in the most conveniently located Christian school, for the single reason that they were black," he says. "My innocence [over the lack of racism in the world] was replaced with anger and a sense of injustice." This sense of anger and injustice stayed with Steigenga as he served at Lawndale and then as interim pastor at Garfield Chapel, across the Eisenhower Expressway, where the church was in the process of organizing as a CRC, and parents also were trying to enroll their children at Timothy.

Throughout, Steigenga was troubled by the racism that he saw being perpetuated. As he served the churches in Chicago, Steigenga entered into the lives of his parishioners and offered them what he could, encouraging them in their effort to find a home for their children at Timothy. In the process, he learned the sobering lesson—one he carried from then on—of what it meant for people to be without social power in the face of those who had it and had no desire to give it up or share it in any way. In other

---

[1]     Calvin Theological Seminary, BD, 1967; MDiv, 1986; ordained 1968; Cherry Hill, Inkster, MI, 1968-74; Nardin Park Community, Detroit, MI, 1974-78; LaGrave Ave., Grand Rapids, MI, 1978-2008; retired 2008.

words, he said, he learned about oppression and institutional racism. He learned of the "racially tinged attitudes that are endemic to a relationship between power and weakness, even if both sides profess to follow Jesus." Like so many other pastors who were part of the battle, Steigenga says it helped to shape his ministry. "Sometimes I wonder how my life and the direction of my ministry would have been different if it had not begun in an urban setting in the turbulent sixties," he said. "However, I wonder not with regrets but with gratitude to God for those experiences. This side of glory, losing innocence is a part of growing up."

After serving Garfield, Steigenga left to be the minister of congregations in the Detroit area and ultimately at LaGrave CRC in Grand Rapids. But before he moved from West Chicago, he watched in 1968 as the area went up in flames after the assassination of Martin Luther King. He was also there when the struggle that he had joined over Timothy began to grow and take on a life of its own. He was there when, only two months after King died and Lawndale erupted in a riot, the issue exploded and began to consume the entire denomination.

# CHAPTER 14

# The Call for Civil Rights in the CRC

During the Sunday morning service at Ebenezer CRC, in Berwyn, on April 7, 1968, Rev. Eugene Bradford read a prayer relating to the assassination of Martin Luther King Jr., who had been killed three days before as he stood on the balcony of the Lorraine Motel in Memphis, Tennessee, where he had gone to show his support for striking garbage collection workers. Bradford spoke about the violence and the repercussions which occasionally followed the demonstrations led by King. "Let it be remembered, however, that the same thing has happened whenever conscientious men have sought truth and freedom in the day of tyranny and ignorance," said Bradford, who had been called to the church about a year before from Westminster Theological Seminary in Philadelphia, where he served as executive director.

In the letter he read on that morning, Bradford spoke about King's legacy, highlighting the significance of King for those

Eugene Bradford
(*Archives, Calvin College*)

who cared about equality in all areas of society. "It is especially important that we Christians, who are called by our Lord to love our neighbor as ourselves, shall not only appreciate and thank God for advances traceable to Dr. King's influence but shall also increase our prayers and redouble our efforts to promote love and understanding, freedom and justice between black and white people of our beloved but sorely distressed land." Bradford did not specifically mention Timothy Christian on that morning, but it was probably on his mind, said his son, Jonathan Bradford, in an interview in 2015. "When my father came to Ebenezer from Westminster, he had not been especially involved in civil rights issues," he said. "He was familiar with these issues a little from work he had done at a church in Paterson, NJ."

But when Eugene Bradford, who died in 2010, saw what was happening at nearby Timothy, he grew deeply troubled, believing the school board was not acting in a faithful way. He became convinced that God wanted him to join the struggle. "It was apparent to him from the beginning, as much as he wasn't

Jonathan Bradford,
son of Eugene Bradford
(*courtesy Jonathan Bradford*)

looking for controversy, that God had placed him at Ebenezer in a leadership position," said his son.

Throughout the struggle, said Jonathan, and for decades after, his father spoke of the great providence of how God chooses people to do his work in certain situations, and his father was convinced and grateful that God had chosen him to play a role in the Timothy fight. Jonathan Bradford worked for many years as director of an inner-city housing ministry in Grand Rapids.

As one of his first steps in leading the charge against the school board, Eugene Bradford went before his consistory on February 5, 1968, with a proposal asking members to draft an overture about the Timothy School situation, calling it sinful, and requesting that their local assembly of churches, Classis Chicago North, send it on to Synod 1968. Bradford believed it was time for Synod to get involved; he hoped the school board might be swayed if the denomination formally declared its actions intolerable. He also saw the overture as responding to the wider issue of racial discrimination in America.

Bradford wanted the overture to call on Synod, the major annual assembly of the church, to assign a day of prayer and fasting for the entire denomination regarding the racial crisis. He also wanted the overture to seek full fellowship for the children at Timothy; failing that, the school board should be subject to church discipline.

Daniel Veurink, clerk of the Ebenezer consistory and, incidentally, principal of the Timothy Christian Elementary

Ebenezer Christian Reformed Church (*Archives, Calvin College*)

School, put the overture into writing, stating it was an attempt to "glorify God by means of a serious attempt to help in the present racial conflict in America and throughout the world." Although the overture was broad, it touched on issues close to the Timothy conflict, calling on the Christian community, wrote Veurink, to "quickly and determinedly unite in the development of a very careful plan to bring about an orderly reception of Negro children in obedience to the demand of Christ who includes them also in His Covenant of Grace."

Not all members of the Ebenezer consistory favored the overture, but eventually Bradford helped to guide it through. We can speculate that playing a role in the consistory's backing of the overture were memories of a conflict Ebenezer had in the late 1940s in seeking to have its own children admitted to Timothy. At that time, the Ebenezer children were considered by Timothy as being lower-class whites who "brought an inner-city mentality to the school," writes Swierenga in *Dutch Chicago*.[1] But after a relatively short-lived spat, they were allowed to enroll, albeit reluctantly. Although the earlier situation may have touched a chord as the consistory put the overture forward, it was the current struggle that mattered. Bradford and others firmly believed the Lawndale children should no longer have to remain in limbo. The stalemate needed to be broken.

Especially significant in Ebenezer's overture was the request for Synod 1968 to "declare that members of the Christian Reformed Church . . . freely receive as brethren, regardless of race or color, all who repent of their sins and make a credible profession of faith in Christ and [to declare] that the exclusion from full Christian fellowship on account of race or color is sinful." The time had clearly arrived for a wider debate, and, Ebenezer believed, the matter of sin topped the agenda.

After some haggling, Classis Chicago North passed the overture and sent it on to Synod 1968, which had received other overtures as well. Some supported Ebenezer, and others strongly sided with the Timothy school board. Summing up their overture, Ebenezer wrote: "Our community must face the situation with earnest prayer to God that He will make us all sensitive to the crisis which is upon us and that the [Timothy] board and the entire community will be given the necessary insights and courage to follow the mandate of Christ, our Savior-King."

---

[1]    *Dutch Chicago*, 433.

# CHAPTER 15

# An Earlier Struggle Resolved

The Ebenezer overture was part of a synodical process of dealing with the issue of race relations that went back to 1957, at which time Synod was asked to discuss the topic due to an incident that had occurred the previous year at a Christian Reformed church in rural North Carolina. Specifically, a family from the North Carolina church had sponsored a Dutch Indonesian family who had come to the area so the father could work on a local farm. Problems arose, however, after the couple joined the church; the mother was dark skinned. Some church members grew concerned, fearing someone who had a dark complexion would alienate the surrounding community, so wrote CRC pastor Rev. Gordon Negen[1] in his booklet "The Christian and Race Relations." As

---

[1] Calvin Theological Seminary, BD, 1957; ThM, 1965; ordained, 1957; Lodi, NJ, 1957-59; Home Missionary at Harlem, NY, 1959-60, at Manhattan, NY, 1960-65; Manhattan, NY, 1965-69; missionary, Sun Valley Chapel, Denver, CO, 1969-74; ECUM of Denver, CO, 1974-76; Eastern Ave., Grand Rapids, MI, 1976-86; Unity, Prospect Park, NJ, 1986-91; Immanuel, Kalamazoo, MI, 1991; retired 1991.

Rev. Gordon Negen
(*Archives, Calvin College*)

pastor of Manhattan CRC, where Huiner and VanderBrug had served, Negen was a strong supporter of Lawndale, and his church had helped in many ways, such as raising money for the Bluebird bus to take the children to Des Plaines.

Negen writes that the incident over the woman from Indonesia arose when the North Carolina community "was just beginning to take this Christian Reformed church seriously and that the church was hoping to evangelize the community. These members believed that the presence of a black person in their fellowship would end their budding evangelism program." Some in the church, according to Negen, even feared they might have to leave town if it became widely known that a black woman attended services.

Things escalated; the church became so divided, its council decided to suspend offering the Lord's Supper, according to Dick Harms, the CRC's denominational archivist. When the church stopped having communion, the matter caused enough controversy that it went before Classis Hackensack in New Jersey, which had member churches in the South.

Classis sent representatives to investigate the trouble and determined the church was out of line and strongly requested it reinstitute the Lord's Supper, said Harms. "They started offering it again, but a significant minority ended up leaving the church," Harms added.

In bringing the matter to Synod 1957, Classis did not specifically mention the clash at the North Carolina church, but it did ask Synod to issue a statement regarding racial prejudice, which Synod did. Among other things, Synod put together a document, which said in part:

> Negroes have been deprived of rights and opportunities equal to those given to whites, have been often relegated to a position inferior to that of whites in social respectability.
>
> Racial prejudice leading to such social injustice is a tragic blot on our society. It is the duty of the members of the church of Christ to be active in removing this stain. The church is called upon to heal that which is broken and raise up that which is fallen. Therefore, it is called to give special help and nurture to those against whom a social injustice has been committed.

This document went out for response to CRC congregations, as well as to the Reformed Ecumenical Synod, a group of denominations in North America, Great Britain, the Netherlands, and South Africa, of which the CRC was a charter member. The Reformed Ecumenical Synod, based in Grand Rapids, reviewed the material and drew up a twelve-point declaration on race when it met in 1958 in South Africa. The Reformed Ecumenical Synod then submitted its proposed declaration to the CRC's Synod 1959, which reviewed and adopted it, and, in the process, the declaration became the CRC's stand on race relations. Subsequent Synods affirmed and added to the declaration, which in essence still stands today.

Promoting the belief that all people of all colors and races are part of God's kingdom, the statement adopted in 1959 says: "The fact that 'God has made of one blood all nations of men' (Acts 17:26) implies that the fundamental unity or solidarity of the human race is as important as all considerations of race and color." Other parts of the declaration state: "For a believer, the decisive consideration, in determining his relationship with members of another race, is the commandment which God Himself has laid down for all human relations, namely, that we should love our neighbors as ourselves." In addition, it talks about Christ's death on the cross and his atoning for the sins of all people, which "implies that all races are included in the plan of salvation, and called to eternal life (Gen. 12:3; Matt. 28:19). From this it follows that a believer has primarily to regard the members of another race as fellow-sinners, to whom he should bring the message of the Gospel."

Yet another point, and especially applicable to the Timothy Christian School struggle: "The practical implication for the ministry of the Church is that in common congregational meetings and in admitting members of another race to our own gatherings, we should guard against any impression of discrimination which could imply the inferiority of the other race, the members of which should be made to feel that they are being regarded as fellow-members in the body of Christ, bound to us by the closest of ties."

In his pamphlet, Negen writes that the statement of Synod 1959 was a good start on the path to better race relations in the CRC. Synod "not only testified to the unity of the human race but also to the Christian's duty to receive all believers as brothers and sisters in Christ . . . and to guard against any impression of discrimination which could imply the inferiority of another race." But Negen also points out that, despite passage of that earlier statement by Synod, racism still confronted the church in the conflict involving Timothy Christian School and that this was "an even more difficult and complicated situation," which it clearly was.

While the issue in the South was largely about church members being worried about their ability to do outreach, Cicero was another story; white violence could break out should blacks be given the right to enroll. But deeper, beyond Cicero, was the issue of racism. It lived on and festered in the hearts of many Christians, and it was a sin that needed the grace of God to be eradicated, said Negen.

# CHAPTER 16

# A Call to Action

Synod 1968 met that year from June 12 to 24 at the Calvin College Fine Arts Center in Grand Rapids, Michigan. On Friday, June 14, not long after the opening service and other formalities, delegates from all over North America took up the Ebenezer overture; people packed the seats to follow the discussion. Anticipation filled the air, and emotions ran high. Many individuals, after all, had been involved in the bitter battle which began in the summer of 1965. For the Lawndale parents, it had been a tough three years, and they were anxious and uncertain as the matter was brought before delegates. On the one hand, they hoped and prayed Synod would side with them. On the other hand, they were familiar with disappointment, especially when it came to dealing with the hierarchy of this church, which seemed worlds away from inner-city Chicago.

Synod 1968 meeting at Calvin College, Grand Rapids, Michigan
(*Archives, Calvin College*)

Some at the Fine Arts Center backed the Timothy school board, believing it had been falsely accused. Still others in the auditorium simply had a keen interest in the matter. As he sat in the Fine Arts Center, Duane VanderBrug found it hard to grasp the reality that the request of twenty black children to attend a Christian school close to their homes would draw this kind of attention. But as the discussion unfolded, he could see the significance of what he was witnessing, especially in the context of the 1960s. Delegate after delegate rose to speak, some making impassioned speeches, other seeking clarification on the finer points of the issue. Everyone seemed to realize they were dealing with a weighty issue in the context of their denomination, which at that time had 634 churches and a total membership of 278,869. "I saw that Synod was dealing with the crucial issue of racism in our society, and at first we didn't know how the church was going to respond," said VanderBrug. But he soon realized, as it became clear Synod would side with the parents and their children, that his discussion was going to have a wider impact; it would ripple through the CRC in many ways for years to come. It could also serve as an example of one small church bringing forth a big message.

VanderBrug listened as Synod 1968 delegates unequivocally stated that "obedience to Christ or fear of persecution or of disadvantage to [one's] self, arising out of obedience to Christ, does not warrant denial to anyone, for reasons of race or color, of full Christian fellowship and privilege in the church or in related institutions, such as colleges and schools."

Synod also declared, reiterating the words of the Ebenezer overture that, "Members of the Christian Reformed Church ought freely to receive as brethren, regardless of race or color, all who repent of their sins and who profess their faith in Jesus Christ as Savior and Lord; that exclusion from full Christian fellowship on account of race or color is sinful; and that if members are judged responsible for such exclusion, they must be dealt with according to the provisions of the Church Order regarding Admonition and Discipline."

VanderBrug was pleased by what he heard. He saw that placing the Timothy school board's position into the category of sin—and threatening discipline and admonition—was a great victory. It was the best outcome he and the Lawndale parents and their supporters could hope and pray for, regardless of what the immediate future held.

Synod, however, did not stop at declaring the actions of the Timothy school board sinful. It also requested the Christian Reformed Board of Home Missions to "design, organize, and implement programs through which the denomination, individual churches, and members can effectively use all available resources to eliminate racism, causes and effects, within the body of believers throughout the world in which we live." It was a big order, to be sure, but made with solid scriptural backing and the best of biblical intentions. Synod also instructed Home Missions to form a group, currently called Race Relations,[1] to investigate the situation in Cicero.

These were strong steps. Synod had spoken prophetically, asking the school to follow Christ's command to love their neighbors. It spoke about falling into sin and its consequences, although Synod did not spell out what that meant. When they were done, delegates sent the matter back to Cicero.

[1]    www.crcna.org/race.

# CHAPTER 17

# The Timothy Board Reacts

When Synod 1968 declared the decisions of the Cicero school board to be sinful, threatened discipline, and asked Home Missions to consider the situation, members of the school board prepared their response. Although Synod's action did not sway the board, they knew they had to act. First, they set up an August 18, 1968, meeting with Lawndale parents. Albert Kieft, the school board president, nicknamed "Swede," addressed the group.

"We are aware of the situation here in Cicero," said Kieft, as quoted in the minutes. "I am not condemning you people in the least . . . but, at this time, we have a responsibility. These matters press heavily against us. We have taken no action in regards to it, but we realize some day, we will have to. It is our responsibility to our God." Eventually they would have to open their doors to black students, but not just now, he was saying. Meanwhile, the school came up with a plan to gauge the feasibility of admitting black students from the Lawndale area to Timothy. They decided to survey the community, to send out letters and ask some six hundred people to respond and give their opinion about integrating the school. Given Cicero's already racist inclinations, the survey results were not surprising.

Ultimately, 244 replies came in: 13 in favor of the Lawndale students attending and 217 opposed. And there were ten threats of violence in the survey responses. A letter to the editor in *Cicero Life*, published in summer 1968, highlighted one person's reaction: "I see in the paper that Timothy Christian School is going to bring twenty Negro students to attend classes and that they are seeking the approval of the neighbors for this. . . . Where are those twenty students going to eat lunch? Where will they play when other students go home for lunch? People take heed. If you don't put a stop to this mad scheme now, you had better have For Sale signs printed up because you will need them soon afterwards."

Referring to a researcher who examined the survey, Mark Mulder writes that the results showed Cicero residents believed African American parents would eventually want to follow their children to Cicero, buy homes, and "The neighborhood would be ruined." The results also showed that respondents believed that children should always attend school close to their present home; and, integrating Timothy "would present a danger to the children, the Christian school society, and the general populace of Cicero," Mulder quotes.[1]

The school board said the overwhelming number of negative results showed bringing the Lawndale students "into the Cicero community would disrupt the orderly processes of educating the children presently in the Timothy Christian School." According to an article in the newspaper *Berwyn Life*, they also convinced the board that it was "not interested in following through" with any plan for integration.

[1]    *White Flight*, 47.

Results of the survey were released at a meeting of the board in October. Having learned of the meeting through a press interview a few days ahead of time, people flooded into a room to hear the results, recalled Eugene Bradford, who had attended the meeting with Duane VanderBrug. The meeting started as the board president, Albert Kieft, told people that the school was ultimately making its decision that evening based upon what God wanted and not on what the survey found, recalled Bradford in a 1970 letter. Approximately one hundred "angry" people were there, many of them members of the CRC and many of them Kieft's friends, Bradford said. The crowd was not happy, especially when they heard Kieft start off by saying the board would base its decision on what God wanted, not on the survey, which might mean integration of the school. They cried out in protest; it was not a pretty scene.

"I went to the meeting to observe, expecting it to be tense, but not expecting it would be mad, chaotic," says Bradford. He described several people talking at once, shouting down school board members, yelling at one another, crying out. "The devil was very much present, and I, for one, did not intend to dialogue with him."

Trying to gain control of the crowd, Kieft sketched the survey results. He assured them no black children would be admitted to the school, apparently indicating the survey results coincided with God's will on that matter. Also, said Kieft, the survey results were evidence that the school board was on the right track. Finally, the board president told the people not to worry; they would be consulted, should the matter come up again. This started to calm the crowd, and the anger died down. Eventually people drifted out, having gotten what they wanted; they learned what they already knew: Cicero would have nothing to do with integrating Timothy.

Bradford, however, left deeply troubled—not just by the behavior of the crowd but also by that of the board. He remained convinced, and perhaps more so than ever, that the school board members were hiding behind the threat Cicero posed. They could have admitted the children if they had so chosen. The survey was a paper tiger; the results were a foregone conclusion before anything went out in the mail. Bradford was convinced God wanted these children to have the chance to obtain a Christian education. He wrote: "Not only do we believe that was God's will but also that the laws of the United States were clear enough" on this issue, namely, that a school could not keep children such as these out because of the color of their skin.

Believing that "the expedient of barring black Covenant children of the Christian Reformed Church could not be justified because of the anger of racially prejudiced people," Bradford redoubled his efforts to fight for change.

# CHAPTER 18

# Frustration and a Loss of Hope

In subsequent months, the struggle stretched out, moving into 1969 without resolution. Various groups tried to get the Timothy board to change its mind and open the school for the 1969-70 academic year to Lawndale and Garfield students. But board members refused, continuing to make the case that, as a local entity, neither the classis nor the denomination could tell them how to run the school. Behind the scenes, they bristled at Synod's handling of the matter and particularly at its use of the loaded word "sin," writes Swierenga.

During this time, Classis Chicago set up a committee to study the situation and give advice on how to untangle it. The committee did its work, which included looking at the feasibility of Lawndale students remaining at the Des Plaines school. It released a report in January 1969 that brought the matter into focus. The report emphasized that the options for Lawndale parents were running out. The committee said that the Des Plaines school was filled with its own students and could "accept, at best, only a small number of Lawndale children above the present figure of 26, and those would have to be in the lower grades. It can accept no more in the upper grades." In doing their homework, members of the committee also contacted several other Christian schools in western Chicago, asking if they might be willing and able to accept students from Lawndale.

The committee found that those schools, too, were near capacity. In addition, the committee learned that many of the same attitudes as those found at Timothy were prevalent in those Christian schools as well. The schools either could not, or would not, admit blacks, said the classis report. The committee concluded that, only "strenuous, prayerful efforts, through the preaching of the Word of God and by means of personal counseling could overcome the matter of race at area churches in general and in the Lawndale/Timothy situation in particular."

The committee's call for prayer was heeded by Classis Chicago North, which met on January 15, 1969. In addition, given the action of Synod 1968, the classis urged Lawndale parents to apply again to have their children accepted for the fall of 1969, suggesting they write a letter to Timothy to set up a meeting to discuss it.

Dorothy Roberts, secretary of the Lawndale Christian Education Committee, did write a letter on March 16. She was hopeful that Synod's decision about sin could conceivably sway the school board's thinking. She and others hoped the board would now, in good conscience, change course. But the board was still of one mind. About a month after she sent her letter, Roberts heard back from the Timothy board, which said "It would be impossible to accept your children for enrollment in our school at the present time. . . . We assure you that this decision was prayerfully made in a Christian spirit, and we are hopeful you will accept this decision in the same spirit."

The board's response infuriated them, causing the education committee to have Roberts write a letter in May to classis, demanding it start acting with conviction and "to bring an end to this defiance on the part of Christian Reformed members and redress our grievances. It is our conviction that our Lord gives our Covenant children rights which no man may deny." Classis received the letter in May, but did nothing with it. Meanwhile, however, a committee of classis, favorable to Lawndale parents, sent a letter in late May to Synod 1969, informing Synod of the ongoing standoff over admitting black children to the school. This was not a formal appeal or overture but was intended rather as an update to let Synod know that its pronouncements of the previous year had not swayed the Timothy board one bit. The Lawndale consistory also sent a letter stating its case, as well as detailing how the classis had failed to act on the matter.

Synod 1969 took up the matter again and, among other things, insisted that the classis start living up to its responsibility and revisit the issue by holding a special meeting in July. In addressing this matter, Synod expressed "its genuine concern for the problems faced by the Lawndale consistory to meet the Christian educational needs of their Covenant children at the nearest Christian school" and urged "the parties involved to do all in their power to meet these needs—at the earliest possible date."

Synod 1969 then underscored what the church said in 1968:

That Synod declare that fear of persecution or of disadvantage to self or our institutions arising out of obedience to Christ does not warrant denial to anyone, for reasons of race or color, of full Christian fellowship and privilege in the church or in related organizations, such as Christian colleges and schools, institutions of mercy, and recreational associations; and that if members of the Christian Reformed Church advocate such denial, by

Class of 1968, Des Plaines Christian School
(*courtesy Ray Vander Molen, principal
and teacher at Des Plaines Christian School*)

whatever means, they must be reckoned as disobedient to Christ and be dealt with according to the provisions of the Church Order regarding Admonition and Discipline.[1]

We had a seesaw battle taking place—tossing the hot potato back and forth between classis and Synod. If nothing else, it was a war of words—strong words on the part of Synod.

# CHAPTER 19

# A Last Straw

After Synod 1969, classis at first seemed unwilling to act. They held a special meeting in July, just as Synod had asked, and it went nowhere. But then Classis Chicago North showed signs of rallying to the cause. When it met for a regular meeting on September 17, 1969, delegates finally tried to make some headway on the issue by putting forward a series of motions. As the meeting began, delegates expressed hope that classis would be willing to bend and come to a strong consensus on the matter of addressing the issue of sin. It seemed that classis, instead of making lukewarm—if any—pronouncements, might speak boldly. There was hope that classis would finally intervene and formally request the Timothy school board to change course. Classis, like Synod, had no jurisdiction in the matter; it could not force the issue. But so far, it had failed to speak boldly and, at the least,

Rev. George Stob, 1962
(*Archives, Calvin College*)

go on record as opposing the actions of the school board. Thus began that September meeting.

By a margin of 15-11, classis voted to support a recommendation stating "classis acknowledge its guilt and sorrow in failing to act in accord with the declaration on race of the Synods of 1968 and 1969 concerning the Timothy-Lawndale issue." Reasons given for this recommendation, according to classis minutes, include the "disillusionment, heartache, and alienation in our Christian communities," the situation they had caused, as well as the need that classis "must respect the authority of Synod."

Classis also voted in favor of sending a pastoral letter to the Timothy school board imploring it "to no longer countenance [continue to bar] the children of black Christians from its school in Cicero." One of the reasons classis gave for this recommendation, says the minutes, is that "the school board's present policy is not in harmony with Synod's declaration on race."

But then, after a rancorous debate, classis showed how far it was willing to go on the matter—when push came to shove. Expressing sorrow and guilt was one thing, but sending a pastoral letter was another. Things stopped there, though, for the majority of delegates, when it came to branding the school board's actions as being sinful. They voted 18-8 to defeat a motion that said

Professor Howard Rienstra
(*Archives, Calvin College*)

"classis declare the practice of excluding black children from Timothy Christian School in Cicero, out of fear, is disobedient to Christ."

Some delegates expressed exasperation when this went down to defeat, throwing up their hands. James La Grand, pastor of Garfield CRC, was a visitor, not a delegate, to the meeting. Thus, he was unable to register his disapproval on the classical record. He chose to express his anger by walking out in protest. Clearly, the debate over these motions reflected the deep divisions Chicago delegates had. They waffled, leaning one way at first, but then a majority simply failed to take a stance. "Classis Chicago North did wrestle long and arduously with the problem facing her," wrote Rev. George Stob, pastor of Wheaton (Illinois) CRC, in the *Reformed Journal*. "But her formal response was uncertain, without conviction, and somewhat self-contradicting and equivocating."

Howard Reinstra, chairman of a Home Mission subcommittee studying the issue, described the deadlock and disagreement at classis in a letter to Rev. James White, pastor of Manhattan CRC in New York City. Reinstra put it this way:

Rev. James White
(*Archives, Calvin College*)

"The so-called 'Timothy-Lawndale' problem in this classis has given rise to such polarized attitudes and opinions that the very discussion of it tends to be sinful."

# CHAPTER 20

# Momentum Builds

Lawndale parents grew more frustrated as classis and Synod effected no change. Calls for prayer and strong words and more meetings were fine, but the issue remained: their kids could not go to the Christian school next door. Lawndale parents began to feel increasingly betrayed and abandoned. The refusal by classis to identify the Timothy board as disobedient to Christ was a last straw. They sent off letters, powerfully stating their case. Evident in these letters is that their patience had worn thin. Their emotions were frayed. They wanted desperately to see movement take place and change occur.

In one letter, addressed to the race commission in Grand Rapids, Lawndale parents spelled out how they saw their role in the denomination after the inaction—that is, the lack of real change—coming out of Synod 1969 and then the classis meeting in September: "Our place in the denomination is less meaningful than it ever was, and it seems you have withdrawn to let us take defeat alone. We want you to know that we feel even lonelier now than we felt before you came on the scene." Dorothy Roberts boiled down the sentiments of the parents in a letter to the *Banner*: "We are black Christians, members of the Christian Reformed Church. . . . But—and here is our problem and our pain—our Covenant children below the high school level have been denied admission to the Christian school located only three miles from the church."

Starting to show exhaustion, parents in Lawndale released a letter during late summer of 1969, after the failed special meeting in July, informing people that, because things were going nowhere, they were not going to apply at Timothy for the school year. Given that the Timothy board refused to meet with them earlier in the year, and because of other setbacks, they were taking their request off the table. In the letter, they also criticized Classis Chicago North for its ongoing inaction. Despite their pleas, Lawndale parents said in another letter, they were deeply wounded that classis kept refusing, unlike Synod, to categorically "call the policy of the [Timothy] board sinful."

In the letter sent in late summer, the parents pointed out that the CRC's synodically established race commission, created in response to the Ebenezer overture, had fallen flat on its heels. This commission, the letter says, "has been on the scene, and has not produced any change in the situation." The commission tried to meet with the Timothy school board, but nothing but more of the same came of it—lots of talk and little action. Lawndale parents said they wanted to take a break from constantly beating their heads against the wall.

But they did not want to give up. They simply needed to regroup and receive additional help before moving ahead. They could not continue the fight alone; they needed more supporters who would walk with them through this struggle. Above all, the parents said they needed the hope that additional backers would provide support if they were to decide to keep going. "For our own sakes, we cannot afford too many more disappointments," they wrote. "We do not ask you to do a miracle. We only ask you to put yourselves on the line. Don't be so afraid of losing. If Christians will take the right risks, and take them for Christ's sake, then losing can be winning."

For the last three years, the parents said, they had been trying to build momentum on a local level and in the denomination at large. "Through every means [open] to us," they said, "we have tried to make the conscience of our denomination sensitive to the racism which exists in this part of the body of Christ." Passionately written and just as passionately argued, these letters had an effect. People across the denomination were reading them in the *Banner* and elsewhere. Even if the parents did not quite realize it, they were succeeding, and the momentum they sought was building. As the school year for 1969 opened, Christians who supported the parents had begun to mobilize and were ready to act. Even though Lawndale parents had decided not to seek to enroll their children in Timothy for 1969-70, help was in the offing. They would soon get the assistance they requested.

And it would soon bring this struggle into the national spotlight.

# CHAPTER 21

# Taking It to the Streets

Eugene Bradford stumbled out of bed at two o'clock in the morning, on Wednesday, October 21, 1969. His phone was ringing. A "dreadful" ring, he recalls. Who was sick? Who had died? the pastor asked himself. "Hello? Hello?" he said into the phone, asking what was wrong. "Nothing," said the voice on the other end. "Got to get out to Cicero. Get as many people as you can to meet at Ipema's[1] Oak Park apartment for prayer at 6:00 a.m. Teachers, escorted by Rev. Joel Nederhood, are going to resign this morning at 8:30. We are going to be there to support them." In his reflection of that day, titled "Some Thoughts on

[1] Calvin Theological Seminary, BD, 1969; ordained 1975; faculty, North Park Seminary, Oak Lawn, IL, 1975-80; director, Multi-Racial Leadership Development, Synodical Committee on Race Relations, Oak Park, IL, 1980-86; SCOFF, Oak Park, IL, 1986-87; president, Mid America Leadership Foundation, Chicago, 1987-2001; vice president, Council of Leadership Foundations, Chicago, 2001; Timothy Institute, Grand Rapids, MI, 2007; retired 2011. *Historical Directory*, 240; *Yearbook*, CRC (2015), 609.

Rev. William (Bud) Ipema
(*Archives, Calvin College*)

a Chilly Morning in October," Bradford said he had heard that teachers might walk out of Timothy Christian School to protest the school's exclusionist policy, but he did not know when.

After calling Ebenezer's consistory clerk, Daniel Veurink, the principal, to warn him what was up, Bradford climbed into a car with others who wanted to be on hand to support the teachers. Riding into Chicago in that crowded car, Bradford felt a mixture of thoughts and emotions. "Romantic and daring—ah sweet relevance! How like the martyrs. Savor the sacrifice. Count the cost of discipleship," he wrote. This was an important day for him and for others. The teachers, with their supporters, planned to take public action. No more endless committee work, fruitless meetings, and hollow pronouncements. Like so many groups in the sixties, they were going to place themselves in full public view, believing that only strong action, whatever the risk, would get their cause across to the broader public. Come what may, they were taking it to the streets for all to see.

Rev. William "Bud" Ipema, who was working for Young Life in Chicago and attending Lawndale CRC at the time, recalled how a "relatively large group of local individuals and supporters from the Midwest had gathered at our home for prayer and to give support to the resigning teachers" on that morning. Calvin College professors and others from Grand Rapids were on hand

and, in fact, had been traveling to Chicago in recent weeks to pray for those involved in the Timothy controversy. Gathering in homes and at the Lawndale church, they had been sorting through how to best address the fight, and the conclusion many had come to—namely, the resignation of teachers—was happening this morning.

Bradford said there was excited talk, people comparing what time they had gotten up and how long they had traveled to get there, as he sat in Ipema's house. Although there were a few yawns, firm commitment was evident on people's faces. Bradford heard the doorbell ring, and in walked the teachers. He wanted to meet them but realized their eyes were red with tears. They had just seen their students walking to school as they came to this house. The teachers looked distraught, troubled that by quitting, they were abandoning their students. They had, however, prayed about this. They had thought this over together and alone and were adamant about what they wanted to do. "They whispered together trembling," recalls Bradford, "they were going through with it!"

The teachers who quit working at the school that day were: Linda Moseson, Karen Cox, Howard Stob, and Elizabeth Westerhof. All except Moseson were Calvin College graduates. Karl Westerhof, a Calvin seminary student on leave to work at Lawndale CRC, explained the actions of his wife, Elizabeth, and the other teachers to the *Chicago Sun Times*. "The teachers believe it is intolerable for white Christians to deny admission to this school to black Christians."

In an interview in 2015, Elizabeth Westerhof said she had started at Timothy as a fourth-grade teacher at the beginning of the school year. Until the day of the walk-out, she and the other teachers had met every morning before class to pray and discuss the action they would take. "I know it was hard for the kids for their teachers to be doing what we did, but we were calm in our spirit and firm in our beliefs," she said. "We chose to do what we did, not because it was tough, but because it was right. We did it because we felt a strong sense of hope that things could change."

A group of demonstrators from Trinity Christian College in Palos Heights, Illinois, joined protesters from Calvin College and Calvin Theological Seminary and a few others from around Chicago to draw attention to the action by the teachers. Rev. Joel Nederhood, director of the *Back to God Hour*, in Palos Heights, walked in with the teachers to support them when they placed their letters of resignation on the principal's desk. Liz Westerhof remembers seeing a crowd of chanting people—not supporters— as the teachers left the school. She also recalls a car racing down the street, seemingly right at them. But someone stepped in, squeezing them into another car and, according to plan, whisked them to a safe house somewhere outside of Cicero.

Looking back more than forty-five years, Westerhof is not sure how much progress the United States has made on the issue of race relations, especially in light of all of the issues over police violence being highlighted by the Black Lives Matter protesters in 2015 and 2016. But that day in Cicero, in 1969, was a chance to leave a mark, however small, in a struggle that had torn apart her denomination. "We were eager and ready as young people to make a difference," said Westerhof. "I was excited to be a part of it."

Outside the school on that morning, people supporting the teachers took time to pray, and then one person spoke to the newspaper *Berwyn Life*, one of several media outlets on hand, saying: "We are not violent people, so we are using this silent protest march to express our disagreement with the school's policy of refusing to admit blacks." Then they began to walk through the neighborhood. "We took a route past the school and beyond toward the Christian Reformed churches," said Ipema. "As we marched, a crowd of onlookers and angry folk in support of the school board gathered along our route yelling invectives at us. Someone had apparently called the police."

As they walked, they saw the Cicero police ahead and two patrol cars blocking their way. In an email interview, Ipema recalls, "Being in the front of the marchers, I saw the police sergeant standing at his open door talking on his car phone apparently to his captain. I heard him say, 'What should I do with these marchers? Shall I wipe them off the street?'" When he heard the captain tell the sergeant to stop the march, Ipema turned to the marchers and told them to get on their knees to pray, "as we all did." Again, he heard the sergeant address his captain, asking what he should do now that the protesters were praying. The captain told the sergeant to let them pass. When they got up, they moved on, harassed by the crowd but no longer particularly bothered by the police.

The protest march took about two hours; about fifty people participated. The demonstration was peaceful, except for catcalls and some angry, red faces, recalled Bradford.

Protesters sang softly and prayed as they marched. Some people from Cicero actually joined them, but others stood on the sides, and Bradford heard one of them screaming, "Hippies! . . . Why don't you get the hell out of here? I supported that school!" Swierenga writes that, despite the generally peaceful nature of the day, things did "turn ugly" at one point "as parents had come to pick up their children after the principal closed the school. Some parents joined the school janitors and some aroused Cicero residents in heckling the quiet marchers." Otherwise, though, things were calm, if not a little unnerving with all of the commotion. School was closed until the next week when substitute teachers were brought in.

Kieft, chairman of the Timothy school board, was asked to comment on the demonstration and the resignation of the teachers. "I'm so busy finding replacement teachers that I don't have time for it," he told the *Chicago Sun Times*. "I'm making sure our children get a good Christian education." Covered by major news organizations, including a film crew from NBC, the protest drew headlines across the nation and deeply divided many in the CRC who were already in conflict over the issue. The two sides became even more entrenched. Likely, no one's mind was changed—at least not at that point.

The *Daily Iowan*, the student newspaper at the University of Iowa in Iowa City, just across the Mississippi River from Illinois, reflected on the controversy in an editorial, stating, "Substitute teachers have been hired, and the school was scheduled to reopen — without black children present. We feel this situation to be a significant example not only of the church standing aloof from problems of our generation but of actively engaging itself as an arm of oppression."

# CHAPTER 22

# Reactions Run Rampant

Eugene Bradford was one of those who received push back from the protest march. One night, not long after the teachers had walked out, he got a phone call from a woman who said: "Mr. Bradford, you are the one behind the effort to get black children in the school. I live across from the school and when my husband comes home, we're going to organize our block, and you're going to get a bullet through your window tonight." Although he considered it a crank call, he left his home with his family to stay elsewhere for the night just to be safe.

In late October, the teachers issued an open letter to the Timothy school board explaining their position. They called it "an outrageous affront to the unity of the Church when an institution that calls itself Christian persists in a policy . . . [which] destroys the integrity and witness of our denomination." They also made a larger point about the school being segregated. "One of the

Professor Alvin Plantinga
(*Archives, Calvin College*)

great tragedies of this situation is the harm done to the white children who are cut off from fellowship with their black brothers and sisters in Christ at the time in history when this lesson most urgently needs to be learned."

Meanwhile, the teachers received a flood of letters, some in support and others levying harsh criticism. In one letter, a Calvin College professor applauded their "courage and conviction. . . . For I am, too, convinced that Christian obedience demands that we in no way discriminate against our black brothers, that instead, we stand ready to share in their sufferings and humiliations." Alvin Plantinga, a Calvin philosophy professor, wrote: "It is as heartening to see you take this action as it is disheartening to see the school board continue to refuse to admit Christian children to our Christian school."

Another letter came in, criticizing the teachers, based on the same argument that had been used before: enrolling students in the Cicero school would cause them harm. "I believe with all my heart that our board members are Christians, dedicated to Christ and his Kingdom. Their decision has led me to believe they want the best for our Covenant children, and this includes the blacks. If trouble comes with our children in school, then what? Must we jump in the fire to see if we'll get burned?" Yet another supporter of the school board wrote: "We believe that God meant us to be separate. That is why so great a distinction—black and white."

In another letter, the writers—a married couple—talked about their child, a Timothy student, and the fear and confusion their youngster felt on the day the teachers resigned. The couple said the situation was complicated, but the children were the ones who suffered. It was the job of the teachers, they wrote, to teach and not to give dissertations in the classroom about racial matters. In doing this, they wrote, the teachers ran the risk of "terrifying" the children. The couple went on to make a distinction between teachers who walked out and the significance of eventually allowing blacks into the school. They called for patience and prayer, of being aware changes like this take time. They wrote, "Our faith does not tell us that God would stay the hand of rioters but rather that He will let us find a way to let these children into our school in such a way as to bypass the neighbor's opinion or bring them in with their understanding. This is why we need prayer and understanding and not open antagonism."

Not long after the teachers resigned, the Christian Reformed Board of Home Missions issued a press release, asking the church's Committee on Race Relations to call on churches across the denomination on an upcoming Sunday "to remember in prayer our common responsibilities toward our brethren of other races." Rev. Roger Van Harn, a Columbus, Ohio, CRC pastor and member of the Home Missions board, said prayer was necessary and would allow concerned Christians to "demonstrate concern for all persons involved in the dilemma. Without doubt there are school supporters and board members who want to act in faith by opening the school to black children but are paralyzed by fear."

Gwen Bradford
(*courtesy Bradford family*)

Meanwhile, the Calvin College student senate voted to circulate a petition that was a "statement of support for the four teachers who resigned." Overall, the petition pushed for resolution of the issue, "now four years old and with no end in sight." Even as the reaction to the walk-out continued to reverberate throughout the denomination, the resignations at the school were not over: Gwen Bradford, wife of Eugene Bradford, resigned, as did Daniel Veurink, the principal, effective July 1, 1970.

Gwen Bradford's resignation was not, however, in protest; she quit so she could leave with her husband who had been called to another church. Eugene Bradford and the Ebenezer consistory concluded that his activism had stirred up too much difficulty, and they made the mutual decision that he should leave. "Many in the church still supported him and the Timothy cause, but both agreed that he couldn't be effective there any longer," said his son, Jonathan Bradford.

With all the publicity, the state board of education stepped in and said Timothy would likely lose its accreditation for violating federal rules and for barring blacks from the classroom. The Timothy board basically ignored the state, contending state accreditation for a Christian school was not necessary.

# CHAPTER 23

# The Battle Continues

Probably wishing this matter of racism would magically vanish, Classis Chicago North had no choice. Once again, it got involved and addressed the issue but—not surprisingly—did not make much headway.

Minutes to classis and other reports show that classis, as it contemplated how to respond to the teacher walk-out, heard from various people. One of them was Karl Westerhof, who addressed classis in January 1970, sketching out the situation confronting the Lawndale church, in which he was serving as an intern. (Duane VanderBrug had left to take over urban ministry leadership for Home Missions.) Because classis had failed to step in on behalf of Lawndale, there was "sagging morale of the congregation," Westerhof stated in his report to classis, which was quoted in *Chimes*. Westerhof told classis the teens group had disbanded in discouragement; church attendance had dropped, and some long-time members had moved away. He also mentioned comments made by black Christians: "They do not care to invite their neighbors to this church, which is slowly strangled by a white suburban power structure." The church languished, said Westerhof, while classis endlessly debated the issue.

At the same time, however, Westerhof said the congregation was enduring and, ironically, even in some ways holding its own. "I am amazed every day at the seemingly inexhaustible supply of grace and love and patience within the Lawndale congregation;" qualities, he cautioned, that may not last if parents continued to be rebuffed.

Also at this meeting of classis, Ebenezer CRC delivered a protest, sharply criticizing the refusal by classis in September 1969 to call the Timothy board's actions sinful. "Failure to struggle against such a state of affairs is to surrender to the tyranny and dominion of racism and is an evasion of our Christian, communal calling to let 'justice roll down like waters, and righteousness like an overflowing stream' (Amos 5:24)," Ebenezer wrote. But neither Westerhof's words nor the protest filed by Ebenezer made any difference; neither helped to shift delegates away from their stance on the matter. Classis could not—or would not—muster the nerve to institute change. Not unexpectedly, they took the easy way out and maintained the status quo.

And this is what happened, time and time again, during the classis meetings Westerhof attended over the years, said Rev. Richard Grevengoed, who succeeded Westerhof and served for several years as pastor of Lawndale CRC. Classis was divided, and the division meant ongoing inaction. Grevengoed recalled with sorrow attending the endless and fruitless classis meetings. He said, in his estimation, "The reason that classis never censured members of the CRC who were on the Timothy board is that money and power [held on the part of the Timothy board] usually rule when difficult moral and ethical issues need to be addressed."

Barb and Rich Grevengoed (*courtesy Grevengoeds*)

He recalled how the few CRC congregations near Lawndale CRC consistently fought to have the students admitted to Timothy, while most of the churches either remained generally neutral or supported Timothy.

"I remember one classis subcommittee meeting I attended when one committee member challenged a prominent pastor as to why he consistently voted to support the Timothy board," said Grevengoed. "An uncomfortable exchange followed with the pastor admitting that one of the Timothy board members was paying the tuition of the pastor's children."

Grevengoed also remembered how, after numerous overtures, discussions, and defeated motions, "a particularly poignant classis meeting unfolded at the Wheaton CRC. In midafternoon one of the delegates proposed that the discussions should end for the day and a season of prayer, seeking God's guidance on how to best move ahead ought to begin. The delegate was the late Henry Washington, an elder from Lawndale and the son of one of the founding black members of what is now Grace CRC in Grand

Rapids. But Washington was rebuffed, and no formal petition for prayer or further action was taken.

Writing in the *Reformed Journal*, Rev. George Stob said that the position of Classis Chicago North evolved over time from briefly supporting Lawndale in 1967 to siding—if only by its inaction—with Timothy. Through 1968, 1969, and 1970, he wrote, "Chicago Classis North had repeatedly, in official decisions, refused to acknowledge that denial of right and privilege to black children out of fear of suffering was disobedient to Christ."

In the end, Classis Chicago North put together a communication to Synod 1970 which ignored the sentiments of its pro-Lawndale delegates, such as Grevengoed and Washington, and illustrated the position of most delegates, essentially telling synod to stay out of its business. They especially did not like the threats coming from West Michigan. They had the right to do their work as they saw fit without fear of recrimination. Among other things, their communication reads: "The exercise of admonition and discipline is the task of the local consistory, and the authority of the consistories is original, and that of the major assemblies is delegated. Based on this fundamental principle, it is questionable whether Synod has the right to legislate the use of admonition and discipline in a specific situation."

Delegates to Classis Chicago North were basically thumbing their nose at Synod as well as the denomination as a whole. Maybe it was frustration, or conviction, or even embarrassment over the publicity of the teacher walk-out. Whatever the case, it sounded like classis by this point had reached the end of its rope and wanted the CRC to know it. Classis just wanted to be left alone to handle—or not handle—its business, just as it saw fit.

# CHAPTER 24

# The Center Fails to Hold

Delegates to Synod 1970 had plenty to handle in matters relating to Timothy, particularly in the wake of the teacher walk-out. Classis Chicago North was not alone in submitting a communication; many others weighed in on the topic. Classis Hackensack in New Jersey, for instance, sent in an overture, seeking the CRC to use the situation in Cicero as a forum to speak about racism across the denomination. Classis Hackensack asked Synod 1970 "to admonish the churches to engage in intense self-examination, so that the pervasive sin of racism may be identified, confessed, and repented in appropriate ways and so uprooted."

In addition, the Board of Home Missions, in consultation with the CRC's Race Relations commission and a group called the Black Conference, asked Synod 1970 to adopt several resolutions. Significant changes in the church's institutions and procedures were strongly requested. Home Missions came up with resolutions that ranged from asking Synod to include minorities on the CRC's Board of Publications, to creating courses in minority history and literature in core curricula at Calvin College, to changing the Church Order "to permit congregations to sing hymns not in the *Psalter Hymnal*, subject to the discretion of the Consistory."

Delegates to Synod 1970, which met June 9-19, at the Calvin College Fine Arts Center, liked the suggestions from Home Missions and adopted them, helping to chart—or at least begin—a new course for minorities in the CRC.

Synod also took other action, looking favorably on the overtures of such groups as Classis Hackensack. And instead of acceding to Classis Chicago North's request that it be left to handle its own matters, Synod made it clear that it wanted classis to stop talking and start taking action regarding Timothy Christian School. It asked the classis to bring the school board into harmony with the pronouncements of Synod. And then Synod hit hard, declaring boldly that, if there was no change, Chicago Classis North would be considered "in contempt of Synod and in open disregard of the judgment of the Church of Jesus Christ." This was the first time in its history that Synod had threatened to hold a group in contempt of Synod, says Swierenga.[1]

Synod went on to "declare the Church is ready and willing to offer total support should it actually experience spiritual or physical distress in the fulfillment of its obligations to the black Covenant children of its communities." Swierenga writes that Henry Stob, a Calvin Seminary professor of moral theology and advisor to Synod, said "The egregious behavior of Classis Chicago North and the Timothy board 'is calculated to shame us all.'"[2]

Finally, Synod 1970 opened the door to what would be an important development when the next year's Synod—once again faced with Timothy—failed to deal with the matter. Synod 1970

[1]    *Dutch Chicago*, 438.
[2]    Ibid., 439.

authorized its race commission "to assist in taking whatever legal action is necessary to obtain protection of law as may be necessitated by enrollment of black Covenant children in Timothy Christian School in Cicero."

In many ways, Synod 1970 was a watermark time. Unlike Synod of 1969, this Synod put teeth in its words. At the same time, an unfortunate reality emerged. By lodging the contempt threat, Synod was reflecting the growing reality that the fabric of the church was starting to tear. The center, the bedrock of the church, no longer held.

# CHAPTER 25

# Synod Washes Its Hands

After Synod 1970 had acted, chastising Classis Chicago North and threatening to hold it in contempt, local Grand Rapids WOOD TV interviewed Rev. Jacob Eppinga,[1] a delegate to Synod and pastor of LaGrave Avenue CRC, to get his reaction. The general public and many in the church wondered what this meant. It seemed to be a big deal. Splinters were occurring in the denomination that held a powerful and respected place in its hometown of Grand Rapids. To think that it was ready to criticize one of its own in this way was, if nothing else, intriguing to some people and deeply troubling to others. The local media was now interested and beginning to ask questions. "Synod has made a statement in 1968 and also in 1969 on the matter of race," said

---

[1]  Westminster Theological Seminary, MDiv, 1943; Calvin Theological Seminary, 1944; ordained, 1945. Dearborn, MI, 1944-51; Highland Hills, Grand Rapids, MI, 1951-54; LaGrave Ave., Grand Rapids, MI, 1954-87; retired, 1987. *Historical Directory*, 203.

Rev. Jacob Eppinga
(*Archives, Calvin College*)

Eppinga. "Consistency required that we do this. I believe that having made the statement, which is certainly based on Scripture, we must practice what we preach."

The television station also contacted Rev. Gary Stoutmeyer,[2] a delegate and member of Classis Chicago North, to get his response. He declined to be interviewed but released a statement making clear that he was speaking on behalf of himself, not classis. "However," he stated, "I believe that after a brotherly and a very moving discussion and prayers for divine guidance, Synod has spoken decisively on the Lawndale-Timothy matter. I personally accept the judgment of Synod and, upon my return home, will do everything in my power to work for the solution to the problem which has been with us for several years."

Perhaps Stoutmeyer did work hard for a resolution once he came back to his classis, but to no avail. Classis Chicago North, throughout 1970, continued to make no progress

[2]   Calvin Theological Seminary, BD, 1958; MDiv, 1975; ordained, 1958. Prospect Park, Paterson, NJ, 1958-63; Calvin, Holland, MI, 1963-67; Elmhurst, IL, 1967-72; Ft. Lauderdale, FL, 1972-75; Faith, Grand Rapids, MI, 1975-79; Coopersville, MI, 1983-90, Bethany, South Holland, IL, 1993-97; retired 1997. *Historical Directory*, 328.

Rev. Gerrit Stoutmeyer
(*Archives, Calvin College*)

toward a solution. Meetings were filled with acrimony on both sides. Delegates met, clashed over the Timothy issue, and left in frustration. In the end, the pro-Timothy faction once again ruled the day, besting the vocal opposition, and delegates sent a communication to Synod 1971, requesting Synod provide "clarity on the threat to hold the classis 'in contempt' and subject to 'admonition and discipline,'" writes Swierenga. In fact, says Swierenga, many delegates smoldered with anger over the whole business of the possibility of being labeled "in contempt." They could not get over the feeling that they were being treated unfairly. They were simply caught in the middle of a juggernaut, not of their own making, they thought. They did not ask for the furor and could not see which way to go.[3]

But Synod 1971 did not provide much clarity and, in fact, seemed to have lost its bearings on the race matter, writes George Stob in the *Reformed Journal*. By then, he said, people in the church, and delegates to Synod, seemed to be tiring of the

---

[3]   *Dutch Chicago*, 438ff.

issue. How many times could Synod speak to it? For that matter, many delegates themselves—not just the representatives from Chicago—were confused over what being "in contempt" meant. As a result, Synod 1971 dithered and failed to provide a strong direction; Synod essentially punted on the matter. The bedrock belief in pushing race relations in Cicero was no longer a priority. No strong statement, only lukewarm admonitions and repetition of what had already been said by previous Synods. But what did emerge was that the issue of race was losing its urgency—if for no other reason than no one really knew what to do about what was an intractable situation in Cicero.

"The Synod of 1971 has taught one valuable lesson to us all. It is that we are in deeper need in the critical area of race relations and our Lord's call to reconciliation with our brothers than we have to this point acknowledged," wrote Stob, who once served Wheaton CRC, located near Lawndale CRC.

In his opinion, Synod 1971 fell short of what it could have done. By now, he wrote, blasting classis or Timothy would not have done any good. Rather, a different approach was needed. Synod had the chance to do something that might have mattered. It could have owned up to its own shortcomings and turned to God for intervention and assistance. "What Synod should have done was to issue a renewed, pastoral, but firm, courageous, and unequivocal teaching concerning the requirements of the Gospel in the crucial area of race relations, while taking strong corrective action with the situation ethics which apparently prevails in Chicago Classis North." Stob did not spell out what that corrective action should be.

Even so, as circumstances would bear out, the matter was beyond a time when a pastoral discussion about ethics might have made much difference. The time was past when synodical pronouncements on the correct action to take could possibly have swayed opinion and changed the landscape of this story.

"In an anticlimactic finish to the ecclesiastical crisis, the 1971 Synod reaffirmed its theological position vis-a-vis the problem but, through lack of meaningful action, admitted its failure to provide a solution," wrote attorney Case Hoogendoorn in a memorandum describing the impasse and making clear the only reasonable way forward. "Therefore, the Timothy-Lawndale problem has, in 1971, become a legal crisis."

# CHAPTER 26

# The Concerned Citizens

About the time Synod 1970 threatened Classis Chicago North with contempt, trouble began brewing as a group calling itself Concerned Citizens of Cicero and Berwyn formed. This group was loosely affiliated with other concerned citizens councils which had sprung up elsewhere in the United States. They all had the same agenda: to derail integration in schools at any cost, even if that meant violence. According to the Southern Poverty Law Center, the concerned citizens councils were formed out of White Citizens Councils, which began in the 1950s to battle school desegregation in the South.

Although this group supported the Timothy school board's decision, which kept the school segregated, it was no lobbying organization. There was a deeper, more sinister aspect of their work. No CRC members were reportedly part of this shadowy group. Rather, it was filled with a combination of mostly nameless

Rev. Jacob Boonstra
(*Archives, Calvin College*)

instigators from outside the area and racist residents of Cicero and Berwyn. Together, the members of the group harbored a hate-filled, separatist agenda, which promised to steamroll anyone who got in the way.

Rev. Jacob Boonstra, former pastor of First CRC, across the street from Timothy, recalls the strident nature of this group. A staunch supporter of the move to allow Lawndale children to attend Timothy, he had worked tirelessly with others for this to happen, holding meetings at his church and attending meetings at Timothy. In a letter offering his recollections of this troubled time, he remembers receiving phone calls from people calling him the devil for siding with Lawndale parents. But he especially recalled getting a letter from Joseph Pellegrini, the spokesman and president of Concerned Citizens. "He told me I was in hot water and wondered what it would take to get me out of town," Boonstra wrote.

Another letter written by Concerned Citizens and sent to the Timothy school board illustrated how worried they were that the board might change course and accede to Synod's demands which would integrate Timothy. Although there was no indication the board was going to open its classrooms to black students, Concerned Citizens wanted to make their position exceedingly clear, stating "The homeowners and taxpayers of the area are violently against this form of 'forced integration'" and added that the residents "cannot be responsible" for violence if integration occurs, according to the *Chicago Tribune*.

In resorting to the threat of violence and rehashing the argument that Cicero was a tinderbox ready to explode if the Timothy board relented, Concerned Citizens showed clearly who they were—a hate group pretending to speak for all of the people in two communities. With the appearance of this group, something beyond a confrontation within a small Christian denomination was evident. A group representing a deeply troubling dimension of society was showing its face. Concerned Citizens, especially during this tumultuous decade of constant change, was a force to be reckoned with. They could not be ignored.

No reports of actual violence surfaced, but Concerned Citizens had touched nerves and brought the issue to another level, and into the middle of all of this came the legal action.

# CHAPTER 27

# Starting the Lawsuit

Case Hoogendoorn was finishing his degree at the University of Chicago Law School when he attended a social action seminar in March 1969 at Trinity Christian College. Speaking about the Timothy controversy at the gathering were Eugene Bradford; Mrs. Ecta Raines, a black member of Lawndale and a Chicago public school teacher; and Duane VanderBrug. Troubled by what he had heard, Hoogendoorn made a trip soon after the seminar to Lawndale. "He knocked one morning on the church door, introduced himself as a law student, and asked if there was any way he could help," said VanderBrug.

Before long, Hoggendoorn began to spend time in the area, knocking on doors and getting insight into the plight that Lawndale and Garfield parents were experiencing. What they faced in the fight with Timothy stirred a deep sense of injustice in the young law student. A Calvin College graduate, he was a CRC

Case Hoogendoorn as
a law school student
(*courtesy Case Hoogendoorn*)

member who saw racism as sin and a rebuke to the requirements of the gospel. He believed this growing up in Iowa, but a personal experience when he was a young adult profoundly helped to expand and shape his understanding of and approach to matters of race. Even many years after it happened, he still chokes up when he remembers it.

A young black girl was staying for a week one summer with Hoogendoorn and his wife before the Timothy controversy, and they took the girl to the beach one day. "We brought our blanket and picnic lunch and sat down on the beach," he recalled. "After a time, the beach began filling up, but then at one point, I realized there weren't many people around us." Hoogendoorn was not sure what to make of it and strolled down by the shore. At one point, he stopped to look back and was surprised and shocked by what he saw. "I saw this big 'v' of space stretching out from the shore to where they were," he says. "There was a large empty area around my wife and the girl." Staring at that empty space, it suddenly hit him in a way it never had before: what it had to be like to be black and ignored in such a public and painful way. "I'll never forget that day," he said.

Motivated by this experience and others, Hoogendoorn got involved in the issues surrounding the Timothy conflict and eventually offered legal help. He said he believed that going to court, especially in the face of the threat posed by Concerned

Citizens, became necessary. It was the only way to try to remedy the breach of civil rights the parents faced. He knew a civil action would take decision making out of the hands of the CRC Synod and place it in the court of civil authorities, but it had to be done. The state, he came to believe, had to step in to do the moral and—ironically—the Christian thing.

Not long after Synod 1971, which simply repeated the words of prior Synods, with no additional proposals for action, Hoogendoorn was asked on behalf of the newly formed West Side Christian School Association, which lobbied on behalf of Lawndale parents, to consider legal action.

First, in May 1971, Hoogendoorn filed a complaint with the Internal Revenue Service, asking that it take away the tax-exempt status of Timothy Christian School Society. He based the complaint on a recent US Supreme Court decision that required tax-exempt institutions, such as private schools, to comply with all federal laws and the United States Constitution, including that they follow federal desegregation standards.

This complaint got the attention of the Timothy school board and William Buiten, who was then president of the board. The two sides set up a series of meetings to see if they could resolve the matter before Hoogendoorn pressed the issue with the IRS. Meeting nearly once a month through late 1971, Hoogendoorn tried to negotiate a settlement to avoid going to the IRS, as well as having to file a federal lawsuit. As part of their negotiations, the attorney offered to represent the board in a suit seeking an injunction to stop the activities of the blatantly racist Concerned Citizens, which, says Hoogendoorn, "had the same agenda as the KKK." The board, however, was not interested.

Then, in hopes of lessening the Timothy board's fears of what would happen if it opened its doors to black students, Hoogendoorn went before the Cicero city council to seek assurances that police would be on hand, if necessary, to integrate the school. Although the city said the police would help, the board was not interested. Hoogendoorn then offered to obtain the protection of federal marshals, arguing that, in order to make this happen, he would seek an injunction on behalf of Timothy to allow black children into the school. In bringing in the marshals, Hoogendoorn told the board, the onus of integration could be placed on the federal government and removed from school officials. "I told them that the board could throw itself on the mercy of the court without hostile reactions. But the board didn't want any of this either."

At one point during these discussions, board members let Hoogendoorn know police protection would not be necessary, since they planned to move the elementary and junior high school to Elmhurst. The board said to be patient; once they moved, the schools would be integrated. "But I challenged them to begin that move by the fall of 1972 if they really believed they could not live as Christians in all their actions in Cicero. The board, not surprisingly, refused to discuss any timetable," he said.

By July, the Timothy board clearly wanted no part of this negotiation process and William Buiten, board president, labeled the work Hoogendoorn was doing on behalf of the West Side Christian School Association as "blackmail" and "extortion." By late 1971, it was obvious, said Hoogendoorn, "how futile it was to continue discussions." The board had no desire to work with the West Side Christian School Association to seek an injunction and request police protection, to enter into joint legal action against Citizens, or to set a date for the school to leave Cicero. "Having arrived at a point where no new alternatives were being offered or were readily apparent, the West Side Board authorized me to prepare to file a suit on behalf of the parents being denied admission," said Hoogendoorn. After this, he asked his law firm for permission to represent Timothy and Garfield parents and children. The firm gave the go ahead, but requested he do this in his own name and seek the backing of the Lawyers Committee for Civil Rights under Law, a local lawyers' organization that was involved in fighting for civil rights.

Hoogendoorn, James La Grand at Garfield, and the affected parents then began the serious project of organizing the lawsuit against the Timothy Christian School Association through its board members and Concerned Citizens of Cicero and Berwyn.

"James was a wonderful man who believed deeply in this cause. He was a very good friend and provided a great deal of help as we put together the suit," said Hoogendoorn. As they prepared the lawsuit, Hoogendoorn suggested to parents, who had children already enrolled in the high school in Elmhurst, to begin withholding their tuition to get the attention of the Timothy Christian School Association, which ran both of the schools in Cicero and the Elmhurst high school.

Besides showing how serious they were in their effort to sue the school, "The parents also needed to be prepared to seek other options for their high school students if they were to be plaintiffs in a suit against the Timothy Christian School Association," said Hoogendoorn. With this in mind, they signed an agreement with the West Side Christian school board and the administration of Walther Lutheran High School in the nearby West Side suburb of Maywood to enroll the high school students if need be.

Hoogendoorn also obtained an agreement from the Synodical Committee on Race Relations (SCORR), a group formed by Synod to address racism throughout the CRC, to underwrite the out-of-pocket costs of the lawsuit, estimated conservatively at $4,000. "This was in accord with Synod 1970's authorization to take 'whatever legal action is necessary,'" said Hoogendoorn. SCORR sent the first check for $1,000, and Hoogendoorn filed the legal action on October 27, 1971, naming all the individual board members and the president of Concerned Citizens. The suit sought an order forcing the school to admit the children and an injunction against Concerned Citizens to prevent it from fomenting resistance to the requested court order. "Although the suit asked for monetary damages as a typical part of any civil rights lawsuit in federal court, no damages ever were anticipated. Nevertheless, just the request became a major source of denunciation of the lawsuit in the CRC," said Hoogendoorn.

# CHAPTER 28

# Brother against Brother

Filing the lawsuit and the request for damages stirred a fiery controversy in the CRC. Many people disagreed with filing a lawsuit in the first place; they insisted church members should not bring fellow church members into court. It would be an egregious breach of the separation of church and state. Especially, they believed, the church was a sacred place under God, and its own should take care of its own, and believers, in fact, were the ones commanded to cast judgment on a wayward and sin-filled world. Scripture taught as much. These opponents cited I Corinthians 6:6: "When one of you has a grievance against another, does he dare go to law before the unrighteous instead of the saints? Or do you not know that the saints will judge the world?"

But others said this passage written by the apostle Paul needed to be read in a broader context and in the light of the "complete Biblical message," wrote Hoogendoorn in his defense of the lawsuit prepared at the request of the editor of the *Banner*, on behalf of the *Banner* and the Christian Reformed Church. "We must settle conflict amicably. This is the message of the entire Bible," he wrote. At the same time, Hoogendoorn said, Matthew 18 suggests ways to settle disputes. While Matthew says forgiveness is the key, there are steps to take if wronged. Matthew 18:15-16 says:

> If your brother sins against you, go and show him his fault, just between the two of you. If he listens to you, you have won your brother over. But if he will not listen, take one or two others along, so that every matter may be established by the testimony of two or three witnesses. If he refuses to listen to them, tell it to the church; and if he refuses to listen even to the church, treat him as you would a pagan or a tax collector.

Does this mean it is permissible, if proper steps are followed, to take your brother to court? Hoogendoorn said yes. All of these steps were followed before filing the suit. For instance, he said, he had met with the board and offered to help obtain police protection. "We met with them and gave them the chance to change their minds, but they wouldn't do that," he said. In addition, they brought it before the entire church at synod, again to no avail.

Hoogendoorn said that, although neither Paul nor Matthew specifically address lawsuits, Protestant reformer John Calvin does. Hoogendoorn quoted Calvin who "unequivocally states that Paul taught 'the need and right to appeal to the civil courts in many circumstances.'" Regardless of how the Bible is interpreted, deep regret and defeat can arise when a brother takes a brother to court, even when there is no recourse other than to file a civil action, wrote James La Grand in a letter.

"It hurt James deeply to see what was happening, not only to the parents and children at Garfield and Lawndale but also to the entire church as well," said Hoogendoorn. In his letter, La Grand says he much preferred to see the Timothy situation handled within the church. Synod, he wrote, had spoken, and the Timothy school board should have confessed its sin and opened the doors of the school to blacks. He refers to going to court as a defeat for good Christian people, yet nevertheless necessary. La Grand also said it was important to realize, once the matter went into court, it was taken out of the hands of the church, and this posed possibly unforeseen problems. The church and the state are two separate entities. The church cannot really depend on the court making decisions for the good of any Christian group. "We must pray for the wisdom necessary for the effective exercise of spiritual judgment even in the default [defeat] itself," he wrote. Whether the judge ruled for or against Timothy, the court will have spoken, and the church would need to accept that decision. "The case in court is not and was not intended as a test of the church's judgment," he wrote. "This must be repeated and remembered. If the judge interprets the civil law in such a way as to offer no protection to the parents, the church's judgment should still stand."

La Grand was a staunch supporter of keeping the church separate from matters of state whenever possible, arguing that the church loses when it cannot resolve an issue itself and needs to go into a civil court, said Hoogendoorn. The Synodical Committee on Race Relations (SCORR) wrote an article for the *Banner* saying that it was also aware that the legal suit could lead to difficulties for the church and that it was "an event that is controversial and likely to generate intense feelings." In backing the suit, however the outcome, SCORR wanted it to be known that "The committee deeply regrets that such a decision should even have had to be considered, but we believe the decision we have made [in writing the $1,000 check to file the suit] is the right one." Going to court, SCORR argued, was the only approach to take if Timothy was not going to open its doors to blacks. It all led to this. Every other move had failed.

As it turns out, SCORR and its members took a great deal of heat for their stance. Even Synod 1970's authorization to take legal action was not sufficient to shelter SCORR from controversy. When word got out that SCORR was providing funding for the lawsuit, it quickly became clear that Race Relations would have difficulty spending more than the $1,000 it had already sent to support the the lawsuit.

"For the next few years, the denomination was determined to deal with the issue of its own synodically created Committee on Racism using its own ministry share dollars[1] to support a lawsuit brought by members of the CRC against members of the CRC," recalls Karl Westerhof, who served as director of SCORR. "Strong opinions were expressed . . . SCORR's funds were frozen for a time," he said. "Subsequent Synods debated whether SCORR should continue to exist. SCORR's budget was cut by approximately 30 percent."

When SCORR was called on the carpet for writing the initial check to fund the lawsuit, Hoogendoorn said he realized he would have to turn to his law firm for help. "They stood firmly behind me and assured me it would cover all additional out-of-pocket costs." As he reflected on those circumstances, Hoogendoorn said, "While Synod's pronouncements were beyond reproach, its stomach for any action left much to be desired. But the lawsuit was filed, and $1,000 toward initial filing fees did come from the Christian Reformed Church in North America through SCORR, which suffered for it in the end." The federal court set a hearing date after the case was filed. Then all eyes turned, albeit very briefly, to the courtroom.

---

[1]    Ministry shares are the apportioned funds churches give to the denomination to fund its ministries. [Ed.]

# CHAPTER 29

# A Day in Court

Lawndale parents soon learned their lawsuit was not going to unfold as they had hoped. Not long before the matter went before a judge, the Timothy school board put its school up for sale, with plans to move it to Timothy's Elmhurst campus. If the sale went through, and the school left Cicero, the case would be moot.

Hoogendoorn said he thought filing the suit forced the school board's hand, causing them to put the school building on the market. Likely, they had a buyer in mind. But since there had been no formal sale by the time the first court hearing was scheduled, the two sides did meet in court, but only once, as it turned out. This dispute would have created a fair amount of fireworks if the two sides had fully argued their cases in court, but that did not happen, because after the hearing, it was learned that a buyer had signed a purchase agreement. A transcript detailing that hearing offers a window into the ending of the conflict.

Here is how it went. As soon as they appeared in court, attorneys for the Lawndale parents said they were bothered by the prospective sale, indicating they thought it was yet one more way for Timothy to avoid integration. "We argued that it was improper for the school to move simply to avoid accepting blacks," said Hoogendoorn, who had help from two lawyers from his firm who had experience in civil rights cases. "We wanted the court to address this matter of the school wanting to move to avoid integration and issue an order prohibiting the move and require that Timothy immediately enroll black children."

But US District Court judge Hubert Will put it this way: "If Lester Maddox wants to go out of business in a particular neighborhood, the people in the first neighborhood can't complain that he is going to be farther away in his new location." Lawndale attorneys realized that the law could not prohibit someone from selling one place and moving to another. Still, they went on to argue that selling the school looked like a ploy and, once the court case was dropped, Timothy might not move and keep to its discriminatory policy. "I think . . . that might be highly unchristian, and I would think it was, but I don't think it is illegal. I think they ought to go to hell for it but not to jail [for putting their building up for sale]," said the judge.

Will told attorneys he clearly saw discrimination in this case. He said, "Nothing I read in the complaint . . . as to why the Cicero situation is different, the tensions in the community, and so forth . . . is not justification for unconstitutional discrimination." But the likely sale of the school changed everything, making Lawndale parents realize that they were defeated. Even so, they asked their attorneys to bring up another issue: the tribulation Lawndale parents would face getting the children to school in Elmhurst, some twenty-two miles away, once the elementary school moved. It was already clear, should the school move from Cicero, that the doors would be opened to blacks—just as the high school had been for years. Although he could not prevent the school from moving, the judge said he might be able to require Timothy to provide free busing for the children. There was no formal ruling on this issue, but the provision of busing became part of a consent agreement, and Timothy continues to provide this type of transportation to this day.

Once the attorneys for the Lawndale parents had had their say, the attorney for Timothy sought to defend the move, saying Timothy had an eye on the future since it was being buffeted by troubling urban trends. The attorney also gave a little history of the school. He said, "In connection with the sale of the Cicero school, these people have [a] good faith, long-range program which started back in '59 which is in process." It was at this time that Timothy moved the high school to Elmhurst. Upon completion of the new elementary school, said the attorney, they hoped that "they will be able to more effectively provide education not only to their own members but also to the black members. This is what is really the heart of this case."

The attorney also said that moving was as much a matter of survival as anything else for Timothy. The school was located in a declining urban neighborhood, faced with the reality of well-to-do white people—those who could afford the tuition—moving out. It could not survive in its current setting. The Eisenhower Expressway had cut through the area; home values were starting to drop, and crime was on the rise. "The membership at this school has declined by about 50 percent over a period of years," said the Timothy attorney. "The people have moved from one area to another. This is not something that started in 1968, or '69, or '70. . . . They have bought this twenty-two-acre campus for a campus, based upon a legitimate and proper consideration."

The judge acknowledged the trends but said he would not accept the line of reasoning laid out by the Timothy attorney about why the school needed to move from the inner city.

Staying right where they were would likely be the courageous and Christian thing to do, said the judge. The initial hearing ended with agreement to pursue the lawsuit once each side was better prepared. But the court case never resolved the matter since the school was soon sold. Should the case have gone forth on the grounds of discrimination, it might have broken new legal ground. "A case like ours eventually went to the US Supreme Court, which ruled in favor of the position we were arguing," said Hoogendoorn.

# CHAPTER 30

# Timothy Today

Today, more than forty years later, Timothy Christian School is in many ways a model of integration, and it has done a great deal of work to make this the case. The numbers show the difference. Nearly 25 percent of the students are from ethnic minorities. Ironically, if "the Christian Reformed Church wants to know what its annual Synod should look like, it should have a look at the playground of Timothy Christian School in Elmhurst, Illinois," opens a spring 2014 article in the *Banner*, written by news editor Gayla Postma. "As I walked around the school, peeking into classrooms from preschool to grade 12, it is obvious that in this student body of more than 1,100 students, racial diversity is a given. It . . . is a far cry from the school that has been held up by the CRC as the antithesis of racial reconciliation for 45 years."

Jonathan Bradford, son of Eugene Bradford, recalls being given an alumnus award, and he was asked to speak at the high

Timothy Christian School Campus, aerial view
(*courtesy Timothy Christian School*)

school a few years ago. "When I looked out at all of the people, I was amazed and very grateful to see this rainbow of colors," he said.[1] VanderBrug said that Bradford himself was a model of civility in the 1960s when he attended the high school. Like his father, racial diversity and acceptance were important to him; color was not a barrier. "Jonathan was the only white student who would say 'good morning' to Barbara Campbell when she got on the bus to Elmhurst High School," said VanderBrug.

But that was then. Timothy today is not what it was; it has many programs linking it with other schools in the inner city. Some of these specifically connect with Chicago West Side Christian School. It is important to remember that the highly integrated

[1]    EB to CM.

Timothy of today is the result of those trends highlighted in the courtroom in 1972 by the attorney for Timothy. Located in working-class Cicero, some thought it was in a dangerous place for black students, as the school board members had been saying all along. And then, as the neighborhood changed, and things became difficult for many in the area, as the attorney for Timothy had told the judge, the school needed to move. It could not sustain itself in Cicero. Instead of taking a stand and choosing to integrate, it left. And although those memories are in the past, and people have moved on, there are still events worth recalling.

Interestingly, said Hoogendoorn, the town of Cicero purchased the Timothy Christian School building for $400,000 and decided to devote it to special-needs children. The attorney said it is his understanding "that it applied for and received federal funds for the programs which served both black and white special-needs children, being an obvious requirement of any federal funding." This being so, said Hoogendoorn, he finds it ironic that, in the end, the school building, located in the heart of racist Cicero, became home for a program that freely accepted blacks and whites and that the federal government helped pay the costs.

Reflecting on the school and the board members he had sued on behalf of the Lawndale parents, Hoogendoorn mentioned both the threats to his career and the reconciliation that happened quietly over time. His three children eventually attended Timothy Christian High School. "That fact still brings tears to the eyes of the principal serving in the high school at the time of the lawsuit and now retired," said Hoogendoorn. "He doesn't miss an opportunity to speak of God's grace when he meets me."

While some board members and former friends never again had any contact with him and his wife, several of the board members and the children of some of the antagonistic board members became friends and clients of Hoogendoorn and supporters of Chicago West Side Christian School, where

This building of the West Side Christian School also serves the Lawndale Christian Reformed Church, which worships in its auditorium/gymnasium (*courtesy Kara Wolff*)

Hoogendoorn had chaired the board for many years. "The whole situation was very painful for many people, but the church learned important lessons about how we should be treating all of God's people," he said.

# CHAPTER 31

# The Light in Lawndale

Reconciliation is what Chicago West Side Christian School has been about since it began as a kindergarten in the 1970s. In early 2016, reconciliation took the form of a basketball game between students at the school and some members of the Chicago Police Department. The game was organized after a West Side teacher took students to meet with police officers at the nearby district office. Students talked to the police about their work, and then they scheduled the game.

The game occurred at a time of festering racial tensions in the community following the release of a video in November 2015 showing Chicago police officer Jason Van Dyke shooting Laquan McDonald, a young black man, sixteen times. It took more than a year for Chicago politicians, who happened to be in the midst of a close mayoral election at the time of the shooting, to release the video. When it finally came out, at the same time of other much-

Mary Post (*left*) and Jeralyn Harris, coprincipals of CWSC, 2016
(*courtesy Mary Post*)

publicized police shootings of black men, social media went wild. News of the graphic video showed up everywhere, and people, many of them members of Black Lives Matter, took to the streets to protest the shooting and how long it took to release the video.

I happened to be in Lawndale, a couple of miles from where the shooting took place, on the day after the basketball game between the police and students. When I got there to do interviews for this book, teachers and students were smiling and excited that the game had made it on three local TV stations. They had shared clips from the television coverage on Facebook, email, and Twitter, proudly showing the spirit—as seen in the game—that has defined this school.

"Everyone is really happy about it," said Mary Post, who serves as coprincipal of the school with Jeralyn Harris. "This is an example of the kinds of things that our school has done over the years—we want to do what we can to help heal problems in our

Pastor Wolff Beginning his sermon on Ephesians 5
(*courtesy Kara Wolff*)

community. We want to bring people together."[1] She mentioned examples of how the school holds programs for neighborhood youth, offers its grounds for gatherings, opens its doors for meetings, reaches out with arts and poetry events, and regularly has students meet with residents of a nearby nursing home.

When she took me on a tour of the school, I saw the auditorium where Lawndale CRC now meets, the gym where the kids and cops played basketball, the lunchroom, and the classrooms where students were busy doing their work. In the library, Post introduced me to two students working on a computer, over which hung a large painting of nineteenth-century abolitionist Harriet Tubman. She also showed me the well-tended area outside where the children have recess. She spoke of how parents and others had hauled donated playground equipment out there and, in one happy day of activity, put it all together for the students.

[1]    MB to CM.

Around 1976 the Westside Christian School took
up residence with the Lawndale Chapel
at 1241 Pulaski Road (*courtesy Kara Wolff*)

As we walked through the school, she said West Side had
struggled for several years as classes were held in the basement of
Lawndale CRC, which still met at that time across the street in
former Nathaniel Institute.

But parents persevered, refusing to give up, believing deeply
that a Christian school was needed in this part of Chicago. In the
early 2000s, they held fundraisers, and in 2004, they opened the
new school, which now has a student population of more than
190, made up of more than 70 percent black children, 14 percent
white children, some Hispanic students, and about 10 percent
students of mixed race.

"We are the most diverse elementary school in this
neighborhood," said Post. "We see this as a safe place for the
kids. I think the families see this school as a huge treasure and
a blessing." At the same time, however, she said Lawndale is a
rough area. On the day I was there, the school had to be locked
down because of a reported shooting in the area. Also, during the
morning, I watched as police cars arrived across the street to break
up a fight between female students of an alternative high school.

Sheila Brooks (*courtesy Mary Post*)

Still, I could see what Mary Post meant: the brightly painted school seemed safe and inviting. The students and teachers I met smiled and greeted me warmly. This was as much a school as a home away from home. Learning was happening here, as was the transformation of lives.

Later in the morning, I spoke with Sheila Brooks,[2] who is now an elder at Lawndale CRC and who raised three sons in the neighborhood. She attended Des Plaines Christian School and then Timothy Christian High School, but her children attended West Side. For a period of time, she said, she had lived an unstable life, but the school was always there, serving as a rock of comfort and a strong foundation for her children. Similarly, Lawndale CRC was there for her when she needed it. "Even when I was out there in the world, something was aching in me, and I kept coming back," she said.

In thinking about the basketball game between police and students, she said it was a great way to show people that this school and the church are all about reconciliation. It also made her consider the complex relations between police and people such as herself in the neighborhood. "It wasn't easy for me raising my sons in Lawndale," she said. "There were times when the police

[2]    SB to CM.

Jim and Kathy Wolff (*courtesy Wolffs*)

weren't anyone's friend, but then there were times when you saw them save someone. I can say that they made a safe pathway for my sons."

She appreciated the fact that the police were willing to show up for the basketball game and to see what was going on at the school. "I believe the church and school have done good things for Lawndale, and this was one way to let people know about that." A few weeks before the basketball games, Rev. James Wolff,[3] pastor of the congregation for nearly thirty years, told church members during a Sunday service that, regardless of what had happened on the night that the young man was shot sixteen times, God loved both Van Dyke, the Chicago police officer, and McDonald, the victim. Wolff told me on the day that I visited that reconciliation—and seeing things from different perspectives—is definitely the message Lawndale seeks to convey. We are all—sinners and saints alike—members of God's family.

As for the basketball game, Wolff said it offered the police a "soft landing"—an opportunity to show a different side of themselves in the current climate of distrust and protest. "They didn't have anyone screaming at them when they came here. It is an example of how we function, of reaching out to people and working to build bridges," he said.

Wolff came to the church in the late 1970s, at a time when resentment still lingered on the part of those who had fought to keep Timothy segregated. But over time, he has worked with

---

3    James Earl Wolff, Calvin Theological Seminary, MDiv, 1978; ThM, 1979; ordained, 1981, Lawndale, Chicago, 1981-; *Historical Directory*, 390.

Rev. Reggie Smith
(*Archives, Calvin College*)

people, smoothing over the harsh memories and eventually bringing people from suburban churches to serve as volunteers at the church and the school. He recalls how one of the fiercest critics of Lawndale parents came down and helped to maintain the church, then in the former Nathaniel Institute, and today the site for an active neighborhood outreach run by a member of the church. Wolff also recalls how Classis Chicago North, which had failed to fight for integration at Timothy, ultimately began to help fund the work of Lawndale CRC and to become a staunch supporter of the school.

"I saw my role as working for healing," he said. "I went out and preached in the suburbs. Back then, there were still hardliners who had a lot of anger and bitterness over what happened. But then over time people got behind the church and the school."

Rev. Reggie Smith,[4] who served as pastor of an inner-city Grand Rapids CRC for twenty years, grew up just around the

---

[4]   Reginald Smith, Calvin Theological Seminary, MDiv, 1992; ordained, 1993; Northside Community Chapel, Paterson, NJ, 1993-94; Roosevelt Park Community, Grand Rapids, MI, 1994- ; *Historical Directory*, 322.

corner from Lawndale CRC. Although he went to Chicago public schools and did not go to West Side Christian, he says simply the presence of the school and especially the church in the neighborhood had a significant impact on his life. Smith is the third of seven children. His father was a steelworker. His mother stayed at home to care for the children until a divorce forced her to take jobs in Chicago factories.

In many ways, Lawndale CRC offered welcome stability. First drawn by the chance to play basketball at the church, Smith got to know church members and grew close to Wolff, learning from him how God blesses the lives of all his children, regardless of their circumstances. Barbara Campbell—"Miss Clayton," as he calls her—served as an important force and role model in his life as well. She took him and other students on many trips and outings, showing them their city. Smith recalls how young people who attended the school and church became close friends. Their parents, especially during church activities, nurtured and engaged him in many ways. "They helped to build the confidence in me so that I didn't have to succumb to the unholy trinity of gangs, drugs, and death," he said.

Wolff worked with him, convincing him to attend college in Missouri and then go on to Calvin Seminary, where, despite many challenges, he earned his MDiv. "People from Lawndale implanted in me a love for God and to make a difference. They taught me about being involved in both word and deed," said Smith. During seminary, he worked for a year as an intern at Lawndale CRC; he also spent time teaching at West Side.

As part of his ministry at Roosevelt Park CRC in Grand Rapids, Smith helped to launch a range of outreach efforts, including a neighborhood arts center, affordable housing units, and after-school programs for youth. Throughout, he used Lawndale CRC as an inspiration. West Side Christian School was also on his mind. His church was a strong supporter of Potter's

Karen Trout CWSCS teacher
(*courtesy Mary Post*)

House, a Christian school next to the church. "I'm so proud of Lawndale CRC and the school," said Smith. "They could have left Lawndale because of the drug traffic and gangs. But they stayed as a countercultural voice of hope, letting us know that it was not all for naught, because they are still there, doing the work and doing it well."

During a break in my day at West Side school, I wandered the halls and checked out an amazing display showing projects that students had completed explaining how cells work in the human body. One after another, the exhibits were creative and informative. In fact, they astonished me with their precision and detail and taught me things I had not known. I wondered which teacher had assigned this project. I soon learned that it was Karen Trout, the eighth-grade science teacher. She also happened to be the person who coordinated the basketball game. She did that because she saw the conflict over the shooting and wondered what small role the school could play in addressing it. "Our heart has been torn over all of the negative energy that came from that shooting," said Trout.[5]

When the video of the shooting appeared, protests broke out across the area. Trout, who has lived in Lawndale for twenty years, took part in some of them. But she also grieved the fact that police officers who work hard in often difficult circumstances were being shown in a bad light. Already having a connection at the local police district station, she contacted them to see if her eighth-grade students could come over and talk to the police, asking about the challenges of their work. "They gave us an hour of their time," said Trout. "They couldn't talk about police procedures, but they shared openly and were vulnerable."

Two days after the meeting, the basketball game was held in the large gymnasium of the school. "It was really great. There was a mad love for these cops when they walked in the door," said Trout. "There was a vast sharing of joy. There were lots of high fives." The kids and the cops played three-on-three at first and then ended the afternoon with a full-fledged, full-court game with students and police officers on each team. Cheers and yells and foot-stomping on the bleachers filled the air. Officer Jamil Brown, who works for the Chicago Police Department, told one of the TV stations, "You want to have CPD show the community that—you know what?—we care."

Near the end of the day, I talked to Clarence "Doc" Taylor, whose father was a key figure in the fight to integrate Timothy. He was practicing keyboard in the auditorium for the upcoming Sunday service. He, too, was pleased the school held the basketball game. His sister is a Chicago police officer. He told me it is important to remember that there are always people who do bad things—and sometimes that person is a cop. "Think about that,"

[5]    KT to CM.

Lawndale CRC praise band in prayer, with pastor James Wolff
and "Doc" Taylor at the keyboard (*courtesy Kara Wolff*)

he said, and I did. And it is true; we all fall short. We all need God's
grace and redemption. Without these, we cannot grow closer to
Christ. It was an important lesson to remember.

When I left school that day late in the afternoon, I found
myself smiling. The Chicago traffic was, as always, crazy, but I felt
really good. Waiting in a long line of cars to get on the freeway
for home, I thought of how Chicago West Side Christian School
is a shining example of what emerged out of the very painful
struggle over Timothy. It is a beacon of light in an area that still
struggles in so many ways. It is a school that serves as a safe haven
amid the chaos of urban America. It a place that, rooted in its
neighborhood, faces problems and does not ignore the issues of
the city—the basketball game was evidence of that.

Above all, I thought, it is a school that reflects the best
biblical principles and fruit of the spirit that can define a Christian
school: love, acceptance, kindness, perseverance, diversity, and
wisdom in what it does. Given the pain the Timothy Christian

School situation caused, this school that coordinated the game with the cops, stands for us as a beacon of light, sweeping across our world and showing us what people of faith can do when they dedicate themselves to issues of education and racial unification. My only regret is that I wish I had been there a day earlier to see that game.

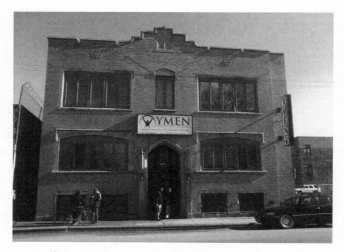

Built in 1927 as the Nathaniel Institute at 1240 Pulaski Road, this building was later transformed into the Lawndale Chapel of the CRC, which became an official church in 1963. In 1976 the Chicago Westside Christian School joined them in this building. Church and school continued here until the new building was completed at no. 1241 across Pulaski Road; building no. 1240, now owned by YMEN, continues to provide office space for the church. The Young Men's Educational Network is directed by Mike Trout who attended Lawndale CRC and is a Wheaton graduate. The building continues to serve the family of Christ (*courtesy Kara Wolff*)

# CHAPTER 32

# Conclusion: God's Grace at Work

Although they finally have their own school at West Side, it is important to remember that the Lawndale parents back in the 1960s were caught in social trends, defeated by racism in the fight with Timothy. They wanted their rights, and they were denied. They fought back and won self-respect and the chance to attend their own school, and yet they also fought back and lost; they were not able to integrate the school three miles from their church.

And this is where our story goes well beyond the trends of the time. Along with being about the troubles of urban America in the 1960s and touching on educational issues and achievements in the twenty-first century, the story underscores the topic of race in the CRC. In this story, we see that the Christian Reformed Church, in facing a thoroughly stubborn school board, began a process of change which continues today. Different communities and initiatives came out of that time; churches were founded, and

Rev. Esteban Lugo
(*Archives, Calvin College*)

other schools were begun. Opportunities in the church opened, first for blacks and then for other minorities.

Many people, however, say that there is still a long way to go; the Timothy situation was less an aberration than an exemplification of a mindset of sin and human brokenness which is as alive in many quarters today as it was then. Certainly there have been successes, and hope remains strong. But a sobering reality remains: progress—deep in people's hearts—is hard to measure. Still, the Timothy story is a concrete example of a determined church and its people sincerely struggling over core values. To say it has reached where it needs to be, this side of heaven, would be far off the mark, many believe.

As he reflects on the Timothy school struggle, Rev. Esteban Lugo,[1] former, long-time director of the CRC's Race Relations ministry, which traces its heritage to the Timothy struggle, says the fight for integration clearly served as the catalyst for the CRC

---

[1]    Esteban Lugo, ordained, 1978; Spirit and Truth Fellowship, Chicago, IL, 1977-87; Spirit and Truth Fellowship, Philadelphia, PA, 1988-92; Bethel, Shiprock, NM, 1992-93; Principe de Paz, Phoenix, AZ, 1994-98; Orangewood, Phoenix, AZ, 1994-98; CRCNA, director, Office of Race Relations, 2004-16. *Historical Directory*, 273.

to focus more fully on the issue of race. Even so, it really is a matter of the effort of reconciliation just beginning, since fighting racism remains an ongoing ministry of the CRC. Racism may not be as overt today as it was at Timothy Christian School, but it remains alive and well in the CRC and in society at large; it exemplifies the fall that sent Adam and Eve out into a broken world. The universe that God made as good and as a welcoming place for all, remains a dream. We get glimpses of God's kingdom—of his full justice and mercy—only sporadically. Redemption brought by Christ leads the way, pointing us in the right direction, and yet we will not get there until the time of Revelation. Meanwhile, we may pause to celebrate our victories, just so long as we realize we still have work to do. "The dismantling of the sin of racism in the church and society is long and hard work," said Lugo.[2] "Racism is a systemic problem, and our approach must be one that deals with it systemically. Only in the process of time, and with intentional efforts of building cross-cultural relationships, will we be able to see the barriers begin to come down." To be sure, however, there are successes.

Back when Lawndale parents were fighting to get their kids into the Cicero school, the CRC had few predominantly multiethnic congregations. In 2016, more than 10 percent of congregations considered themselves to fit in that category. For that matter, when Synod 1968 ruled initially on the Timothy case, the vast majority of delegates were white. In 2014 the number of nonwhite delegates topped 20 percent, a record. These numbers, and others reflecting a slow but growing inclusion of minorities in high-level ministry positions, show that the struggle at Timothy mattered. Today, as opposed to back then, the CRC is a denomination of many faces—black, Asian, Hispanic, Native American, and more.

---

[2]    EL to CM.

Rev. Duane E. VanderBrug
(*courtesy Christian Reformed
Home Missions*)

Clearly, the Lawndale parents, by taking a stand and sticking to it all the way into the courtroom, helped to make this happen. They did the CRC an important service at that crucial time in the church's history. Although there is much yet to accomplish, the story of the Timothy Christian School is one that shows the best and the worst of the CRC. But it is particularly a story about church growth and hope in God. This is a story where the church, guided by the sovereign Lord's presence, started to take a new direction. "I think it was a crucial time, and now, through it, we can see an evolution of perspectives," says Jonathan Bradford, son of Eugene Bradford. Back then, he says, the church was caught in the middle of a racial "tornado," in which people who relied on God's will were "diametrically opposed." But through a series of circumstances and the courage of some people, including Jonathan's father, change occurred, more so in personal attitudes than in the school. "We see in this story how the unfolding of God's reconciling love turned sin and hurt into love and acceptance," said Bradford. "We see how God gave folks such as my dad and several others a role to play in helping to manifest his kingdom here on earth."

Advocates such as Peter Huiner, Duane VanderBrug, Eugene Bradford, James La Grand, Case Hoogendoorn, and others point us to who we are and who we can be. They are examples of a deep reality, the ongoing human quest for unity. They remind us of how we can step up and cleanse ourselves of the things that divide us. They remind us of how the church can reflect the best of who we can be as God's people. They remind us that, as we read in 1 Peter, we all have the opportunity to be part of "a chosen people, a royal priesthood, a holy nation, a people belonging to God, that you may declare the praises of him who called you out of darkness into the wonderful light!"

# Epilogue

Joe Ritchie
(*courtesy Joe Ritchie*)

    The 1960s were at once exhilarating and frustrating. It may be the decade that defined the future shape of race relations in America more than any other in the previous century. Certainly, today's Black Lives Matter movement, which emerged out of the shootings of young black men in the United States, can trace its roots back to that time.

The civil rights movement of the 1960s not only accelerated the dismantling of the most extreme Jim Crow practices in the country but also unleashed powerful backlash forces. It was an exciting era in which to come of age, but for all the true progress of that era, however, there were always setbacks, events like the assassination of Martin Luther King and of the Kennedys; the Birmingham church bombing; and the ambush of civil rights activists like Viola Liuzzo in Selma, Alabama, and in Mississippi, the killing of James Earl Chaney, Mickey Schwerner, Andrew Goodman, and Medgar Evers; and the shooting of James Meredith in Mississippi, who survived.

In no arena were the events of the sixties more pivotal than in the field of education. The fight over desegregating schools, particularly in the South, was carried out at many levels as the Supreme Court's 1954 Brown vs. Board of Education ruling served notice on communities that unequal education needed to be addressed, and the sixties movement gave impetus to challenge segregation in the schools. Across the South, black students began to seek enrollment in higher education institutions like the Universities of Alabama, Georgia, and Mississippi, among others.

Images like those of governors Ross Barnett and George Wallace personally blocking access of black students into their assigned schools are, in many ways, seared into the memories of those of us who grew up in that time. (Less is said about the Georgia governor, Ernest Vandiver, who, despite earlier strong support for segregation, moved to ease the desegregation crisis at the University of Georgia; we remember more a successor, Lester Maddox, who kept a group of black students from Georgia Tech from entering a restaurant he owned by brandishing an ax handle.)

Joe Ritchie, Calvin College freshman
(*courtesy Joe Ritchie*)

But despite all of the turmoil surrounding public school desegregation, especially in the South, what transpired in Timothy Christian School in the Chicago area in the sixties never quite seemed possible to me. In many ways, my own family was wrapped up in the events, though I was not personally directly involved. At the time the Lawndale parents were ready to press to allow their children to enroll in a Christian school, I was already enrolled at Calvin College. Calvin in those days was not exactly a model of diversity; in a student body of from three- to four thousand students, one could count the black students on two or three hands during my four-year tenure at the college. Access, however, was never an issue.

For me, personally, it was ironic, since I had attended Tilden Technical High School in the South Side of Chicago's Back of the Yards area. "Tech" was easily the single most diverse public high school in the city; I know, for I used to study the demographic tables published in the newspapers every year. Until Tilden lost its "tech" franchise midway through my sophomore year, it usually showed black and white enrollment nearly dead even in the low 40 percent range. Sometimes there would be a few more black students; sometimes whites formed the plurality. The census called Latinos and Asians "other," and Tilden had very healthy numbers of especially Mexican Americans and Chinese Americans, but there was also a sprinkling of Japanese Americans, Puerto Ricans, and a couple of Palestinian Arabs; for their part, the white kids covered all the major and minor national ethnic groups of the South Side: Polish, Lithuanian, Latvian, Serbian, Irish, Italian, and so forth. We even had a Dutch guy, Val DeYoung, who was a pitcher on the baseball team.

Yes, I thank God that Tilden Tech postponed my foray into Christian education, for I had valuable contact with peers from all kinds of backgrounds during my formative years. My sister, on the other hand, was one of the three Lawndale students first admitted to Timothy High. Fortunately for her, she only had to endure, and I choose the verb carefully, her senior year. She felt ostracized—shunned even—from day one. There is at least one hero in this tale, fortunately, John Huisman, the center and star player on the Timothy basketball team and a true student leader. One day he apparently had seen enough of the treatment the three Lawndale students were subjected to, and he strolled over and sat down next to my sister in the lunchroom. Because he was (with his height, quite literally) a BMOC (big man on campus), his gesture at least rendered it okay to be civil to the Lawndale contingent. My sister still did not make many friends there, unlike at the public school she had attended in her junior year. She still says it was a miserable experience.

The story may seem trivial, but to me it was one of the two or three things that have stuck in my head about Timothy over the years. It puts into perspective some of the arguments that were always given about why Lawndale children should be denied access to Timothy's Cicero elementary school. Yes, perhaps parents did have real concern for the safety of their own children in a school located in a neighborhood noted for being hostile toward black people. But her experience suggested to me that there was also simply a lot of resentment toward the Lawndale students and perhaps a fair amount of racism.

As for Cicero's reputation, it was well deserved. Berwyn, however, a suburb to the immediate west of Cicero, with similar

Joe Ritchie, Calvin College soccer
(*courtesy Joe Ritchie*)

demographics and a similar reputation, offered another experience. In any case, I managed to make the soccer team at Calvin, despite having precious little experience in the sport. Chicago, however, had a well-organized National Soccer League with amateur teams that usually had direct ties to one or another ethnic community. I called the league office, seeking another team I could practice with in the evenings, after I would get home from my summer job in the summer. (Thanks to one of my Mexican classmates I already occasionally kicked around with the Atlas club from the Pilsen neighborhood.) A league officer referred me to the Sparta club. When he told me it was in Berwyn, I gulped and told him, "Uh, I think I need to tell you something; I'm black." His answer was basically, "So what?" Did I want to play soccer or not? These guys will be happy to let you play. Yeah right, I thought; a bunch of blue-collar Czechoslovaks (it was still one country) in one of the most racist by reputation suburbs in the city. His "so what" answer turned out to be spot-on. Miro Rys Sr., a former two-sport professional star in Czechoslovakia who had just arrived in the

Chicago area that year got me on the field, and everybody seemed happy to welcome me into their circle. (I even got to experience Rys' prodigy son, who at twelve was good enough to play with the seniors and later made the pros but died in a car accident in Germany when he was a young player for the Hertha Berlin club.)

What does this prove? After all, my experience in Berwyn came after the main struggle over admitting the Lawndale elementary students to the Cicero school; by then they were already off to Des Plaines. So perhaps it does not prove a lot, other than that there were people of good will even in Berwyn—and probably Cicero— and, although the neighbors might have been hostile to a civil rights march demanding open housing in their community, I could not see people attacking children trying to go to a privately run Christian school. I am naïve; I had seen the potential for mayhem in the near western suburbs close to firsthand when the Congress of Racial Equality marched on Cicero Labor Day weekend in 1966 and was met with bricks and bottles. I have never discounted that factor, but the attitude of Reformed Christians who had successfully inculcated our community with the desire to pursue Christian education was baffling and disappointing.

One of the most extremely disappointing episodes, something most difficult for me to swallow, was the role of the school board head, Albert Kieft. I knew Albert Kieft in a special way. He was my Sunday school teacher at Lawndale. Well, one might say, does that not show he was committed to supporting Lawndale? I do not know; I do not know what motivates a person to volunteer to teach Sunday school in an inner-city mission. I do know that from my perch at Calvin, when I read the full Calvin College *Chimes* and other accounts of school board sessions, as well as the quotes of my old Sunday school, I was very deeply disturbed.

The one Sunday school lesson I best remember, Kieft was teaching the story of Shadrach, Meshach, and Abednego in the fiery furnace, from the book of Daniel. These were role models for Christian bravery, standing up to Nebuchadnezzar and the forces of evil; this, however, was not the behavior of the Timothy school board or the parents from the west suburban Christian Reformed churches. It would be no exaggeration to say the actions of my former Sunday school teacher presented me with one of the most severe tests of my faith in my entire life. And I do not think I was alone in that. The Lawndale parents stuck to their guns, though, despite the deep disappointment many of them felt at the attitude of their Christian Reformed brethren. These are Christians? What about Shadrach, Meshach, and Abednego? Shallow words. Shallow teachings.

I doubt that many of the Timothy parents ever thought much about the impact their posture had on their brothers and sisters of the covenant who lived just to the east of them, in the North Lawndale community. That the folks at the Des Plaines Christian School were willing to admit the Lawndale elementary students at least showed that there were good people in the church who were ready to do the right thing. And by all accounts, since all of the schools have moved out to Elmhurst, things at Timothy are a lot different these days. I truly hope that this volume may serve as a guidepost to true Christian leadership. There are certainly lessons to be learned from the history of Timothy Christian School, and perhaps a hard look at some unvarnished truths from the historic 1960s will be an instructive teacher. In many ways, times are easier on the race front, although there are still many disturbing signs in our communities that there is hard work to be done. When there are challenges that seem as great as Nebuchadnezzar's fiery furnace, I surely hope that for the Christians who read these pages, Shadrach, Meshach, and Abednego will represent more than a dramatic Sunday school yarn.

Professor Joe Ritchie
(*courtesy Joe Ritchie*)

*Joe Ritchie retired from Florida A&M University in 2013 after twenty years as the Knight Chair in Journalism; he is a former copy editor for the* International New York Times *in Hong Kong and former adjunct professor in the Journalism and Media Studies Centre of the University of Hong Kong.*

# APPENDIX

# Chronology

## 1965

April 14
Lawndale's pastor calls Timothy Christian School president Al Kieft to ask for a meeting regarding twenty-one students who had requested admission to the school in Cicero.

June 22
Meeting with executive committee of the Timothy board. Students are not accepted. Reasons given orally: danger of violence and some CRC members would withdraw support. The executive committee would, however, appoint another committee to arrange an alternative in Lawndale.

July 20
Letter delivered to the Timothy board which agrees with the decision of the executive

committee, as well as that it was too late to act for Sept. admission.

Aug. n.d.    Letter of Timothy board to Lawndale: Your decision is wise.

Aug. 31    Letter of Lawndale to Timothy board asking for written statement of reasons its request was turned down.

Sept. 14    Letter from Timothy board to Lawndale quotes from board minutes which gave no reasons.

Sept. 15    Classis in response to request from the Lawndale church for help, asks churches in Timothy area to work toward progress.

Sept. 30    Letter from Lawndale to the Timothy board asking for clarification of their mention of helping Lawndale get something going in Lawndale.

Nov.    Letter from Gordon Negen, pastor of the Manhattan Christian Reformed Church in Harlem, New York City, reports they had written the Timothy board asking if discrimination was involved and received back a quote from Timothy board minutes which gave no reason.

**1966**

Jan. 20    Lawndale meets with Timothy board committee. It requests that Lawndale students be admitted to the Timothy Christian High School in Elmhurst, Illinois, which is under the same board.

| | |
|---|---|
| March | Timothy board committee reports to the Timothy board. Lawndale project would not be feasible. Children should be enrolled at Timothy (Bardolph, De Boer, LaMaire, Schuurman, Van Denend, and Vander Werken). |
| May 17 | Five Lawndale students accepted at Timothy Christian High School in Elmhurst, Illinois (pending formal approval of grades). |
| Sept. 6 | Lawndale Christian Education Committee (CEC) formed at Lawndale to handle tuition payments. |
| Sept. 7 | Lawndale decides to request help from classis with its problem of providing Christian education for their covenant children. |
| Sept. 14 | Classis Chicago North in reply to Lawndale's request refers it to the consistories for reaction, to reply in time for the January 19, 1967, meeting of classis. |
| Oct. 28 | Mrs. Dorothy Roberts, a Lawndale Church parent, applies to Timothy board for her two children to enter the Timothy Cicero Christian School. |
| Nov. 10 | Lawndale Christian Education Committee gives $63 to the Timothy Loyalty drive. |
| Nov. 17 | Timothy board replies; it is impossible to admit Mrs. Robert's two children. |

**1967**

| | |
|---|---|
| May 17 | Vander Ark of the Nation Union of Christian Schools appraised of the problem and points out that the National Union of Christian |

Schools has no jurisdiction in local Christian Schools.

Jan. 13    Classis Chicago North meets. After hearing from seven consistories, adopts Lawndale overture, appoints a committee, which reports that the Lawndale children should immediately be admitted (Revs. George Stob and Fred Van Houten and elders Veurink, Kief, and Vegter).

Jan. 25    Lawndale pastor Duane VanderBrug meets with Mr. Ottenhof, vice president of the Timothy board, who agrees to keep the lines open, and also to contact Mrs. Roberts personally.

Feb. 14    Lawndale Christian Education Committee contacts Des Plaines and Western Springs Christian Schools re: possibly enrolling their children in their Christian Schools.

Feb. 22    Western Springs replies that it will meet with the Lawndale parents. March 22, 1967.

Feb. 28    Des Plaines replied favorably.

March 17    Lawndale CEC writes Timothy board, asking them to re-examine their policy of not admitting the Lawndale black children to the elementary school.

April 13    Lawndale Christian Education Committee (CEC) requests formal admission of their children to the Des Plaines Christian School.

April 13    Des Plaines board replies: a delegate from the Lawndale CEC may be present at their May 9 meeting if they wish.

| April | A lengthy report with specific action suggestions from Duane VanderBrug, Lawndale's pastor, to the Classical Home Missions Committee on his ten-week study leaves (Jan. to mid-March) with Urban Training Center for Christian Missions funded by a Ford Foundation stipend. |
|---|---|
| May 16 | Des Plaines Christian School Board gives formal approval for admitting Lawndale (and Garfield) children. |
| May 17 | Classis meets and recommends to the church that an offering be taken for the purchase of a bus for Lawndale CEC. |
| July 13 | Lawndale CEC sends an appeal to the churches for gifts to help buy the bus. |
| Sept. | Nineteen (19) Lawndale children enroll in the Des Plaines Christian School. |
| Nov. 16 | The Young Peoples Society of the Ebenezer CRC in Berwyn, Illinois, appear at the Timothy board meeting, asking that the children of Lawndale be admitted to the Timothy Christian Elementary School in Cicero. |
| Nov. 22 | A resolution of thanks was sent by the teachers of the Illiana Christian School in Lansing, Illinois, to the Des Plaines Christian School Board. |

**1968**

| Jan. 15 | Timothy board communication to the Timothy faculty defends and reaffirms its stand against admission of the Lawndale children to the elementary school in Cicero. |
|---|---|

Jan. 27   Lawndale CEC has figures on bus purchase: $7,389 total collected. From six (of 10 asked) churches in classis $1,373; from the Manhattan Christian Reformed Church in Harlem, New York City, $415.

Feb. 5   Ebenezer Christian Reformed Church in nearby Berwyn, Illinois, overtures the Synod of the Christian Reformed Church for a day of prayer and fasting in the racial crisis, for all members of the CRC to be admitted to full fellowship, and those who exclude to be subject to church discipline. The church recirculated the decision of Synod 1968 re: race relations.

March 14   The Rev. Jacob Boonstra, pastor of the First Christian Reformed Church in Cicero, Illinois, protest to the Timothy board re: its exclusion policy.

Spring   Some seventy Timothy graduates ask the Timothy board to admit the Lawndale Children.

April 11   The faculty of Timothy petitions, and Timothy board to appoint a committee to improve attitude in the area.

May 21   The Rev. Duane VanderBrug, Lawndale's pastor, contacted Calvin College re: placing student teachers in the Des Plaines Christian School.

May 24, 31   Two articles on the struggle written by the Rev. Duane VanderBrug titled, "Up the Up Staircase," were published in the *Banner*, the official magazine of the Christian Reformed Church.

| | |
|---|---|
| June | Synod in substance adopts Ebenezer CRC's overture (see Feb. 5 above) |
| Aug. 14 | Timothy board committee has sent out a poll to some six hundred Cicero neighbors. |
| Aug. 18 | Cicero LIFE reports on open meeting held re: admitting the Lawndale children. Albert Kieft, president of the Timothy board: |

> We are aware of the situation here in Cicero. I am not condoning you people in the least . . . but at the same time, we have a responsibility. These matters press heavily against us. We have taken no action in regards to it, but we realize that someday we will have to. It is our responsibility to our God.

> A petition signed by ca. five hundred in the Timothy school neighborhood opposes integration of any Cicero school. Stanley Stava, a Cicero neighbor spoke: "My house is my god. I have 20K invested in that house, and my house is my god."

| | |
|---|---|
| Aug. 26 | Patients at Pine Rest Hospital in Grand Rapids, Michigan, contribute $16.95 to the Lawndale Christian Education Committee for the bus purchase. |
| Oct. | The Timothy board committee reports on poll results to the board. Six hundred residents polled: 244 replies equal 13 pro, 217 opposed, and 10 threaten violence. The poll for Christian Reformed people, through the churches, went aground—sent to the churches but never returned. |
| Sept. 18 | The Lawndale Christian Education |

Committee, through the Lawndale Church council, asks classis' advice, since Des Plaines could not handle additional Lawndale and Garfield enrollments in 1969.

Sept. 26    Twenty-six children (21 Afro American and 5 Anglo), all members of Lawndale and Garfield CRC, re-enroll in the Des Plains Christian School.

Nov. 23    The board of the Roseland Christian School on the south side of Chicago was contacted by the Lawndale Christian Education committee re: enrolling children in that school.

**1969**

Jan. 15    Classis Chicago North meets. Its committee urges the Lawndale Christian Education Committee to try again, urges continuing conversation. The committee is to continue to September 1969 (members: the Revs. Morren, Eugene Bradford, Garrett Stoutmeyer, Schuurman, Mr. Martin LaMaire, and Mr. Van Abbema).

The committee notes that Western Springs is as bad as Cicero. Roseland probably would take the kids, but it is eighteen miles each way through very heavy traffic.

Feb. 5    Roseland Christian School Board replies that it will enroll the Lawndale children.

March 10    Lawndale Christian Education Committee requests a meeting with the Timothy board at the earliest convenience.

March 28    At the meeting, the Timothy board tells the

Lawndale Christian Education Committee: "We can't enroll Lawndale students because of our location in Cicero."

| | |
|---|---|
| April | One Lawndale Presbyterian parent, two from the Garfield Christian Reformed Church, and several from Warren Park have applied. |
| April 17 | Report said that the Timothy board had no intention of changing its policy. |
| May 5 | The Lawndale Christian Education Committee again appeals to Classis Chicago North for help. |
| May 21 | Classis plans to meet. Its committee recommends strong action—without specificity. |

# Index